BFI TELEVISION MONOGRAPH

# 1

6.50

**Structures of
Television**

Nicholas
Garnham

produced by
The British Film Institute
Educational Advisory Service

British Film Institute
127 Charing Cross Road, London WC2H 0EA
1980

In this revised edition of the first monograph in this series, Nicholas
Garnham brings up to date his analysis of the organisational structures of
British television. His account of the present system makes it clear that
broadcasting is an institution which can only be understood both in terms of
its own specifically determined political, social and ideological problems and
in relation to wider issues of social, and especially economic, policy. The
monograph ends with an entirely new section on the implications for
broadcasting structures of the Annan Committee's Report.

**The author**

Nicholas Garnham is Head of Media Studies in the School of Communications at the Polytechnic of Central London. He has written a critical study
of the work of *Samuel Fuller* (Cinema One series) and was co-author with
Joan Bakewell of *Television: The New Priesthood*. He has contributed articles
to many journals, including *Screen* and *New Society*. He has made several
films for BBC Television and was until recently a member-governor of the
British Film Institute.

First published 1973
Revised edition 1978
Reprinted       1980

# Contents

# Introduction (1978)

The first edition of this monograph was written, as I think the text itself makes clear, within the context of a specific debate and as an intervention in that debate. It was also written within and influenced by a particular intellectual climate, the influences of which, while being no less important, are perhaps less apparent. That is to say I would wish to stress the historical nature of this text, as of any other.

In preparing a second edition I felt it was important not to erase the traces of the text's own history because these traces, when foregrounded, help to reveal important developments in the continuing debate about broadcasting structures. In so far as I would wish my original analysis to stand, there is no need to alter what I originally wrote, and in so far as I think I was wrong, the nature of that error and its significance can only be revealed if the reader is aware of the true nature of that error as part of a whole structure of argument. For that reason I have made only minor corrections to the body of the original text. I have excised completely the short section on Existing Alternative Structures, because the lesson of that section was simple, namely that other societies not dissimilar from ours, that is to say sharing a mixed economy and the institutions of bourgeois democracy, have different broadcasting structures, which leads one to assume that there is nothing theoretically sacrosanct about our own. In addition much more work on foreign structures is now readily available, some of which will be referred to in the reading list. Apart from that I have framed the original text with this Introduction, in which I will comment on the text itself, and with a Postscript in which I reconsider certain central structural questions in the light of the Report of the Annan Committee. In particular I have tried in that Postscript to correct the major fault of the original monograph, namely its failure adequately to deal with the ways in which broadcasting is structured economically. For this reason I have also excised the original short section entitled Finance and Frequencies.

This absence of adequate economic analysis in the original monograph reflected a continuing absence in the debate about and research into broadcasting, at least in Britain; an absence in its turn marked by Annan's failure to confront and analyse the economics of broadcasting and thus their failure to make defensible proposals for structural change. A political economy of British mass-media urgently needs to be written and my brief comments in the postscript are obviously no substitute for that work, but they are, I hope, the beginnings of a corrective, signs of which exist even in my original text, to the predominantly idealistic form in which the broadcasting debate is conducted, as much among marxists and socialists as among liberals.

The idealist element in my original approach can be seen in such phrases as 'In the Long Revolution the pen may indeed turn out to be mightier than the sword', in my stating 'the need to recognise broadcasting as a process of communication in which the widest possible range of people talk to each other', in an unthought through notion that 'small is beautiful', that 'we must build our new structures from the margin in to the centre'. This residual idealist strand in my argument was part of that post '68 mood out of which I wrote. The stress on the political importance of ideology and the superstructure in general and of communications in particular, which focussed my concern and was one of the strands of politico-intellectual debate surrounding broadcasting with such groups for instance as the Free Communications Group and their publication *Open Secret*; all this was a reaction against the previously dominant intellectual tradition on the left which was excessively economistic. At the time it was a valuable corrective, but this reaction, as is the way with reactions, swung too far in the opposite direction. In stressing the autonomous political effectivity of ideological work it neglected the extent to which the institutions of the superstructure were involved in an economic activity. The present danger in the discussion of the mass-media on the left, as a result, is of excessively idealist and theoreticist formulations.

But my original monograph was also idealist in another sense. While I think my original diagnosis of the state and status of the debate over the future of broadcasting was correct, I was clearly ludicrously over-optimistic about the outcome. That optimism was politically necessary, however. Advocates of change must exaggerate the possibility of such change in order to make such change possible. They must claim as likely what in their hearts they know to be unlikely.

But the optimism was not merely of that rhetorical and tactical kind. It was part of the mood of that period in which the spirit of the '60s in general, and of '68 in particular, lingered on. Utopianism was still dangerously, as I now think, in the air. People really did believe, in those dear, dead departed days before the Oil Crisis and the current, persistent economic depression throughout the Western economies, that alternative cultures, life styles and the institutional forms to go with them could be constructed within the existing social formation and alongside the more traditional social forms. Individual and small group activism on these lines was the order of the day. In this atmosphere models of alternative media structures, centred in part around new technologies of portable video and cable distribution, and often based upon ill-understood foreign experiences, went with communes and drug-cultures and Maoism and Che Guevara as part of a glorious and imminent liberated future.

I was always uneasy about the sloppy libertarianism underlying both these models of broadcasting power to the people, as well as the syndicalist variants of broadcaster power which arose at the same time, as indeed I think my text makes clear, especially in Models for a New Structure. Nonetheless I was not as immune as perhaps I should have been to the prevailing ethos, for it was this ethos that led me to go along so uncritically with the demand for a Committee of Inquiry itself. For to expect a solution to broadcasting's structural dilemmas from such a source was precisely to expect a depoliticised solution to what I argued was a political problem. Given the political forces in play and the cross-party, non-political tradition of such Committees of Inquiry, Annan could never realistically have been expected to do anything but support the *status quo*. But meanwhile the existence of the Committee served the dangerous function of taking the debate about the future of broadcasting out of the political arena where it properly belongs. The result has been that consciousness of the issues relating to broadcasting policy is now less developed among our politicians than it was before Annan began its deliberations and the IBA and the BBC in particular have had a breathing space in which to rebuild what were in 1972 their badly damaged political fences. In short, change is further away now than when I originally wrote. However, I believe the need is, if anything, more acute because the technological and economic pressures on our inherited structures have grown immensely and unless we grasp the nettle of planned, willed change, large-scale and uncontrolled change will be, is being, forced upon us.

# Introduction

*History does nothing, it 'possesses no immense wealth', it 'wages no battles'. It is man, real living man, that does all that, that possesses and fights; 'history' is not a person apart, using man as a means for its own particular aims; history is nothing but the actuality of man pursuing his aims.*

Marx.

Any study of the structures of television must contradict that tradition of romantic individualism expressed by *The Economist* (Dec. 11, 1971): 'Of course, in the end it is not the structures which determine the quality of any broadcasting system or service but the people who man it.' Such a view, flattering as it may be to individual broadcasting executives, bears little relationship to the real situation. A stress on structure as the ultimate determinant of individual human actions may appear to induce a helpless fatalism, but in fact the opposite is the case. When one stresses the role of the individuals manning the system, one is tempted to await a Messiah who will come over into Macedonia and help transform the system. As Brecht wrote in a different context, 'Pity the country that needs heroes,' for to await the appearance of such men is to neglect our own responsibilities.

A study of structures should induce not fatalism but activism. For it is too easy to forget that our structures are man made. By studying their creation and functioning we can come to the realisation that they could be different; that if we will it, we can change what we originally created. And the more we understand the way such structures determine individual actions, the nearer our new structures may be to fulfilling those functions for which they were created. As Professor J. D. Halloran has written in the Introduction to Broadcaster Researcher Co-operation in Mass Communication Research, 'It is particularly important for the researcher to look at the question of alternatives, especially where the broadcasting institution has a long established tradition. One of the main tasks of the social scientist is to try to expand the range of choice by drawing attention to alternative policies, methods and solutions. In broadcasting this can be attempted at many levels from national policy to programme schedules.'

Once a policy or practice becomes well established and seems to be working, it is remarkable how reluctant we are to consider alternatives.

This consideration of alternatives is not an abstract problem facing social scientists, but an important contemporary political question. The BBC Charter and the Television Act, due to expire in 1976, are now to be extended until 1981. But by then a major restructuring will be even more necessary and in the immediate future the allocation of the 4th Channel remains a contentious question. So the debate about broadcasting structures is very much on the agenda, and it is a debate of much wider social and political significance than merely the future of the BBC and ITV. As Stuart Hall has written, 'Where controversial issues are concerned, there are always distinct patterns and swings in the structure of public attention. This is the social visibility or social history of social problems. Broadcasting like other mass media exhibits this pattern to a striking degree . . . In each phase, issues of the widest social and political significance have been focused through – and displaced onto – the debate about the media.'

For three years now a sustained and often agonised debate has been conducted, both by those who work in broadcasting as well as interested and informed outsiders, as to what the future structure of broadcasting should be. The signs of that debate are probably familiar to newspaper readers. The public revolt of BBC staff over 'Broadcasting in the Seventies', the increasingly vociferous activities of Mary Whitehouse and her allies, the chequered and stormy passage of London Weekend Television, the demand for an Inquiry into Broadcasting met by the setting up of the Annan Committee, which was promptly disbanded by the incoming Conservative government, the demand for a Broadcasting Council to handle complaints, the controversy over censorship of the news from Ulster and finally the campaign against the allocation of the fourth TV channel to ITV. Like the cracks in the earth's crust after an earthquake, these are all symptoms of a debate at a deeper level about certain fundamental issues, the relation of broadcasting to the public, the relation of broadcasting to the State and the role of the broadcaster in relation to public, State and especially to the institutions within which he has been forced to work. They are also symptoms of the accelerating malfunction and break-up of our inherited structures. It seems to be increasingly clear that there must be major changes simply because neither the BBC nor ITV can withstand the stresses placed upon their structures by the rapidly changing social and political environment in which they must operate.

Media men have a greater tendency than most to be full of their own importance. When one attends meetings at which such people contemplate their navels in adoration or scratch their scabs in guilt, one is tempted to question the importance of the debate. Social scientists remind us that no hard evidence can be found that television really affects anyone very profoundly, a useful corrective to the messianic assumptions of the Pilkington Report that 'unless and until there is unmistakeable proof to the contrary, the presumption must be that television is and will be a main factor in influencing the values and moral standards of our society'. Certainly when watching much TV there is a temptation to write off the medium, although it is watched on average two hours per day per head, as an essentially trivial way of passing the time, regrettable perhaps, but not worth an agonised debate.

But this temptation must be resisted. The current interest in communications is more than just a fashion. The media have become the site of a crucial political struggle. This shift in emphasis has been well described by Raymond Williams: 'From one familiar approach, through traditional politics, we have seen the central facts of society as power and government. From another familiar approach, through traditional economics, we have seen the central concerns of society as property, production and trade. These approaches remain important, but they are now joined by a new emphasis: that society is a form of communication, through which experience is described, shared, modified and preserved.' This new emphasis on communication does not merely join the traditional approaches. In an important sense it contains them within itself. Politics and economics are communication sub-systems. The vote is a message which tells central government what actions we, as individual citizens, think society should take in certain circumstances. To use that vote effectively we are in turn dependent upon accurate information about the options open at any given time. Similarly in the economic sphere the price mechanism is a system of messages to tell producers about relative consumer needs and consumers about the relative availability of products. In both politics and economics the flow of this information is of course seriously distorted, in part through misuse of the mass media by means of advertising and news manipulation. But also by the inability to register our vote more than once every five years and only then on the basis of the vaguest of electoral manifestoes, as well as, in the economic sphere, by monopolies and by the inequitable distribution of incomes. If, in a revealing phrase, money speaks louder than words, the rich can send more messages than the poor and so stand more chance of receiving the desired reply.

The importance of communication and the effect of distorted information flow on the structures of social control has been neglected in the struggle for democracy, in what Raymond Williams has dubbed The Long Revolution. This is in part due to the influence, often unconscious, of Marx's famous formulation, 'The totality of these relations of production constitutes the economic structure of society – the real foundation on which legal and political superstructures arise and to which definite forms of social consciousness correspond. The mode of production of material life determines the general character of the social, political and spiritual processes of life. It is not the consciousness of men that determines their being, but, on the contrary, their social being determines their consciousness.' The new emphasis on communication reverses this hierarchy, so that ideology becomes the main weapon of oppression and carriers of ideology such as the mass media become an important political battleground.

Why should this be so? Because a social system is based upon a pattern of shared values and attitudes and assumptions which are carried from one generation to another by various channels of communication, or media, such as the family, the church and the school. It is these shared values that legitimise a given social structure. In modern mass-society with its high degree both of mobility and of division of labour, the influence of the traditional media has in part been supplanted by systems of mass-communications such as newspapers, films, radio and TV.

In such a society information becomes ever more important. If one lives in a stable rural community the information necessary to lead one's life is readily available from the immediate environment. But now, just as we are dependent in a non-subsistence economy on outside agencies for our food, drink and clothing, so too we are dependent on our communications systems for the information we need to function as social beings. Since the actions we take are to an extent conditioned by the information we receive so those controlling the flow of information through the mass media can to an extent control our actions.

A neglect of this central role played by communications in society accounts in part for a certain sense of frustration, even failure, among those engaged in the long struggle for democracy. The vote has been won and little has changed. The commanding heights of the economy are occupied and a miners' strike is still necessary. The Russian revolution has produced state capitalism run by an entrenched technocratic bureaucracy.

The missing element, the unconquered area, is consciousness. A new consciousness can only be created by the social control of communication. It is this important truth that has been grasped by the Chinese in their Cultural Revolution. They have shifted the political struggle into the sphere of ideology in order to create new patterns of motivation and legitimisation. As Marcuse points out in *One Dimensional Man*, we live in a society impregnated by ideology: 'In a specific sense, advanced industrial culture is more ideological than its predecessor, inasmuch as today the ideology is in the process of production itself. In a provocative form this proposition reveals the political aspects of the prevailing technological rationality. The productive apparatus and the goods and services it produces "sell" or impose the social system as a whole. The means of mass transportation and communication, the commodities of lodging, food and clothing, the irresistible output of entertainment and information industry carry with them prescribed attitudes and habits, certain intellectual and emotional reactions, which bind the consumers more or less pleasantly to the producers and, through the latter, to the whole.'

In such a society the media of mass-communication clearly play a vital role and the control of those media is a matter of central political concern. If we believe in a democratic society, we need to look at the structure of our media and see what changes are needed to bring them closer to those ideals. We need to analyse the way in which the means of production of our consciousness are controlled, so that they can be brought under full social control. Of one thing we can be certain. The media are not neutral in the struggle for democracy. In the Long Revolution the pen may indeed turn out to be mightier than the sword. The outcome of that battle will therefore depend upon which side gains control of the pen.

# Structures of Television

The notion of public service broadcasting is sometimes discussed as though it were a peculiarly British concept, invented by Lord Reith, enshrined in the BBC and then extended and improved, or threatened, depending on your point of view, by the creation of ITV. In fact most countries recognise that broadcasting, using limited public resources in the form of scarce radio frequencies, is a public service. The exceptions to this rule, such as Saudi Arabia, Spain and certain Latin American countries, grant licences as a political gift purely for private profit as the king used to grant rights to taxation or customs dues to favoured nobles. The real and proper arguments concern the best method of serving that public. The dilemma facing any society in its organisation of broadcasting can be briefly stated. How to reconcile within a limited number of outlets the need for the State to make judgements of national priority as to how those outlets should be used, the need of each individual citizen for maximum freedom of choice in his search for personal satisfaction and the need for the broadcaster to express the truth about the world as he sees it. Does the State represent the people and should it therefore control broadcasting directly? Unsatisfactory as they may be, are ratings nonetheless the best way of ensuring that the public's preferences are respected? Can we give the broadcasters freedom without encasing them in an ivory tower subject to the temptations of cultural élitism? Any claim our existing system may have to be the best in the world, as is often claimed, must rest on the assumption that our solution to these problems is the best possible, but any such claim is meaningless as all solutions must be partial and temporary reconciliations of ultimately irreconcilable dilemmas. Where we put the emphasis must depend upon the social and political climate in a particular country at a particular time. Our broadcasting system may possibly be the best for us now, but to claim it the best in the world is blind and empty arrogance.

The theory upon which such a claim has been based goes as follows. By vesting the power to broadcast in two independent public service corporations run by bodies appointed to represent the public interest, we have successfully freed broadcasting from State control; by the device of licence finance we have freed the BBC from crude commercial control and the chase for ratings thus allowing minority interests to be catered for as well as mass pleasures; by the device of competition and advertising revenue under firm public service control we have avoided the dangers of irresponsibility and élitism inherent in monopoly and enabled the public to control the broadcasters not only via parliament and the corporations but also via the exercise of choice. As Sir Robert Fraser, the ex-Director General of ITA, once put it, the creation of ITV enabled the viewer to vote with his switch.

This is the comforting, mythic view of British broadcasting. The reality is rather different. What in fact we have is a system in which two powerful institutions responsible not to the public but to the real, though hidden, pressures of the power élite, government, big business and the cultural establishment, manipulate the public in the interest of that power élite and socialise the individual broadcaster so that he collaborates in this process almost unconsciously.

# Broadcasting and the State

The Beveridge Committee in 1949 asked as one of their fundamental questions, 'What alternatives are there to competition and to Parliamentary control as means of preventing broadcasting from falling into the hands of an uncontrolled bureaucracy?'

In Britain, as in all other countries, broadcasting was created and continues to exist by courtesy of the state. To quote Pilkington, 'In the United Kingdom all broadcasting is in charge of answerable public corporations. There are, of course, two: the British Broadcasting Corporation, incorporated by Royal Charter; and the Independent Television Authority, incorporated by Act of Parliament. These instruments give legal existence to the two public corporations. They do not, however, give them the right to broadcast.' For this a Licence from the Minister of Posts is required. Under the Wireless Telegraphy Act 1949 (an extension of the act of 1904) no one may either transmit or receive radio messages, and this includes, of course, television, without such a licence. This control is in part a technical necessity. There are a limited number of frequencies. These scarce frequencies must first be shared out internationally, both between users, i.e. navigation, the armed services, police, fire and ambulance, radio telephones as well as broadcasting, and between nations. The State is the signatory to the current Stockholm Agreement of 1961 governing these allocations. Britain's allocation of frequencies thus becomes a scarce national asset and central government has, rightly and inevitably, the job of deciding the order of priority for the rival claims for their use. In passing I would note that the claims of the armed services and police are not given adequate public scrutiny.

But what is significant and often forgotten is, as Pilkington put it, 'that a control which derives from the need to ensure the orderly use of scarce frequencies – and is thus technical in its purpose – is applied here for reasons which are essentially social'. Or as I would prefer to put it essentially political. The State has from the start used its powers in a non-technical and restrictive manner to reinforce central control. The influence of the Armed Services through the Imperial Communications Committee was crucial in the early debate about the shape of broadcasting in this country. The attraction for the Post Office of Reith's plan for a BBC monopoly was not only that it avoided the embarrassment of having to decide on what criterion they should allocate other licences, but also that unified central control limited the possibilities of subversion. The licensing not only of transmission, but also of reception, quite unnecessary on technical grounds and only later used as a convenient means of raising revenue, underlines this point. The continued limitation on cable transmission and the action taken to prevent the reception by the general public of local educational broadcasting shows that these powers of control are still actively exercised.

But the State has not been content to allow its power to control broadcasting to rest only on its ability to revoke its licences. As Pilkington again put it, 'In principle the powers available to the Government for controlling broadcasting are, subject to Parliament, absolute'. They appoint and may dismiss at any time the Governors of the BBC and the Members of the IBA. They can force the BBC and the IBA to broadcast any programme or to refrain from broadcasting any programme, subject only to the proviso that the broadcasting authorities can if they wish announce that such an action has been taken.

These absolute powers are so extreme that they are, of course, never exercised and successive governments have been at pains to stress the independence of both the BBC and the IBA in matters of programme content and the day-to-day management of their affairs. The result is that extreme apparent government control goes hand in hand with a lack of real Parliamentary control over our broadcasting institutions. The Minister of Posts is not responsible for broadcasting in the sense that other Ministers are responsible for their departments. He can reply to any public criticism of the BBC or the IBA by stating that the independence of our broadcasting from political control must be respected. Pilkington even deplored the fact that Parliamentary questions could be asked at all. Thus the one occasion the Legislature has to discuss broadcasting policy is when the Annual Report and Accounts are laid before Parliament.

Such a situation must result in either the BBC and the IBA, isolated from democratic pressures, becoming increasingly irresponsible, in the true sense of that word, answerable to no one for their actions and judging the justice or otherwise of these actions by standards of their own creation, or in hidden State control. The theory is that the Governors of the BBC and the Members of the Authority prevent the development of irresponsibility by acting as the trustees for the public interest. As we shall see this theoretical view of these two august bodies is pure myth. What has resulted from the present system is the worst possible relationship between broadcasting and the State, a mixture of irresponsibility and hidden State control. The secret compact between the broadcasters and the state has always been, 'You can be as irresponsible as you like towards the public so long as you play the game by our rules when our interests are involved.'

The confusion in this area is well illustrated by the persistent attraction to those who discuss broadcasting of the mythic notion that finance by Licence Fee reinforces the BBC's independence from government. The BBC has never been financed by a licence fee. It is and always has been financed by money voted by Parliament from the Treasury out of general tax revenue. The money raised from licence fees goes into the general pool. Until 1950 the BBC received a set proportion of this sum, a proportion decided by the government. In 1950 they were granted 100 per cent because of the need to finance TV development. In fact the BBC has seen itself as short of money since the days of Reith. Today, with rapid inflation and a saturated market for sets and thus no automatic increase in the licence revenue, the government's power, constantly exercised, to withhold or delay rises in the licence fee gives them close financial control over the BBC. Their ability to raise and lower the levy gives them a similar sanction against ITV. It is increasingly clear that rises in the licence are only granted as part of an elaborate process of bargaining in which the BBC will agree privately to such conditions as, for instance, the start of a pop-channel on Radio One or the observation of government norms in its wage negotiations.

Backed by these formidable powers, the State in fact exercises a daily influence on the output and general behaviour of the broadcasters. The price of independence has been eternal obedience. The nature of this State control was well illustrated in evidence to the Sykes Committee in 1923, when Brown, the chief Post-Office civil servant, said that the BBC could be 'as partisan as it pleases about political or economic or other questions', but added that if the BBC were really to be as partisan as it pleased, 'I am quite sure that the Licence would never be renewed'. A member of the Committee then aptly described the relationship as one of 'Not censorship, an influence and possibly intimidation'. Reith and the BBC showed early that they would play the game by the State's rules. During the General Strike in 1926 Reith defined BBC policy as follows: 'There could be no question about our supporting the Government in general, particularly since the General Strike had been declared illegal in the High Court [an interpretation hotly disputed at the time]. This being so, we were unable to permit anything which was contrary to the spirit of that judgement and which would have prolonged or sought to justify the strike.' He issued a directive that 'nothing calculated to extend the area of the strike should be broadcast' and he justified this by claiming that 'since the BBC was a national institution and since the Government in the crisis were acting for the people . . . the BBC was for the Government in the crisis too'. Such were and are the limits of broadcasting's political independence. The continuing reality of this situation is underlined by the BBC's coverage both of recent strikes and of Ulster and by Chataway, the Minister of Posts, describing, in November 1971, how he saw the role of the BBC in its coverage of Ulster. 'The BBC has made it clear over the years that impartiality could never mean impartiality between right and wrong, tolerance and intolerance, or between the criminal and the law. No obligation of impartiality could absolve the broadcasting services from exercising their editorial judgement and from exercising it within the context of the values and objectives of the society they are there to serve. The BBC have as trustees for the public to judge not only what is best in news terms, but what is in the national interest.'

# The Accountability of the Broadcasters

This notion of the BBC, and also the IBA, as trustees for the public, is in theory the other side of the coin of political independence. Through the Governors of the BBC and the Members of the IBA broadcasting is accountable, so the theory goes, not to Parliament but to the general public. This is the structural basis for the notion of public service. But from the beginning such a notion has borne little relation to reality. The first Governors of the BBC were not allowed to appoint their Chief Executive. They inherited Reith as Director-General and he used the full force of his incumbency to see that he, and not they, ran the BBC. Since that day the Governors have acted not as watchdogs of the public interest but as a suitably distinguished screen behind which the bureaucrats could hide from inconvenient scrutiny. As part-timers, who were specifically instructed not to have or indeed seek any specialised knowledge of broadcasting, they were inevitably totally dependent upon the advice of those officials they were supposed to supervise. The farcical nature of these accountability procedures was clear by the time of the Beveridge Inquiry, in 1949. This was in part, of course, a function of the growing size of the BBC. In 1935 there was a staff of 2,518 and their actions, even when unsupervised, were not of such central importance as they have now become. They only ran two radio networks and their coverage of news and current affairs was still strictly limited. By 1950 the staff had grown to 11,848 and the growth of the BBC's news coverage during the war had made it more than just a potentially powerful political and social force. Beveridge saw the problem as that 'of devising internal as well as public and external safeguards against misuse of broadcasting power. We have to ensure that whatever authority has charge of broadcasting shall have within it effective organs of self-criticism and of response to criticism from outside in continual operation, shall have within it a force making for increasing devolution of authority, shall have within it a force keeping access to the microphone open to all who are worthy of such responsibility. We have to ensure that, if for any reason these internal safeguards prove ineffective in the broadcasting authority as first established, there shall be effective means, outside the authority, of bringing the failure to light and to correction' and they went on to assert that 'some further measures are required to prevent broadcasting falling into the hands of an uncontrolled bureaucracy, however good the intentions of the bureaucracy'. So they recommend that 'the Governors should have a special organ of their own for keeping them in continuous contact with public opinion, informed and uninformed' and proposed the setting up of a Public Representation Service. This would in effect have given the Governors their own independent secretariat, as Lord Simon, Chairman of the BBC at the time, recommended in his book *The BBC from Within*. This secretariat would have taken over and enlarged the scope of the BBC's Audience Research Department, have received and reported on criticism and also maintained a systematic and continuous review of foreign broadcasting institutions and programmes. Had this recommendation been carried out it might have valuably shifted the seat of power away from the Board of Management of which body Beveridge accurately remarked, 'It might look to some as tending to put all real control in the hands of the officials, sending to the Governors recommendations agreed on by a solid phalanx of officials and reducing them in the main to watching the great broadcasting wheels go round.' Unfortunately nothing was done and since that day the BBC bureaucracy has grown both in size and irresponsibility with the full development of BBC1 and the addition of BBC2.

Pilkington were so mesmerised by the failings of the ITA, at which we shall look shortly, that they overlooked those dangers so accurately diagnosed by Beveridge. Now the Governors head an organisation employing 23,000 people, and Lord Hill, although supposedly appointed as a strong Chairman to control the BBC executives, still holds to the Reithian view: 'I think the Governors should remain what they are, amateurs, who assume a responsibility for what is broadcast, who gain an understanding of how the BBC works, but whose task is to defend the independence of the Corporation, resist the pressures on it and to defend those who work in it.' Some watchdog. It is hardly surprising that such a Chairman, although supposedly heading a body of men who are public trustees, has the gall to write in the 1972 *BBC Handbook* that those members of the public who are interested in the internal affairs of the BBC 'should mind their own business'.

But Beveridge were not content to recommend just a strengthening of the power of the Governors. 'How are the watchdogs to be kept awake?', they asked. 'Who is to watch the Governors?' Among other measures they recommended a regular Quinquennial Review by an independent committee appointed by Parliament. This is a most important proposal. The BBC and the IBA are notably antagonistic to the setting up of public inquiries into their operations, using such phrases as 'Why dig away at the foundations?' or 'Why kill the tree in order to examine the roots?' Sir Hugh Greene has written of the invigorating effect on upper management at the BBC of having to give evidence to Pilkington, but he then draws the odd conclusion that such inquiries should not happen too frequently. Surely one would draw the opposite conclusion.

The BBC and the IBA have tried to forestall outside criticism and build higher the mystifying screen of bogus accountability by appointing various Advisory Councils. The most important of these are the General Advisory Councils. Their usefulness can be judged by the fact that they consist of 60 men and women, chosen by the BBC and the IBA, who have no secretariat or research facilities of their own and meet once a quarter to be wined, lunched and flattered by BBC and IBA officials. Their proceedings are secret. What their advice is, is unknown, nor do we know whether it is ever taken.

Faced as it was by a BBC monopoly, it is not surprising that Beveridge concerned itself with the accountability of the BBC, trying to answer their own question, 'Can we without direct Parliamentary control prevent a chartered monopoly for broadcasting from becoming an uncontrolled bureaucracy?' As they went on to state, 'If broadcasting without competition is to be made and kept as good as possible, if mistakes, inadequacy and bias are to be discovered and corrected rapidly and certainly, the need is somehow to provide a channel, not only for popular but also for expert criticism, from outside. It is not sufficient to trust to the mutual criticism of those within the Corporation. It is not sufficient to trust to discussion by Advisory Committees without making certain that they have all the material they need to be useful. . . . There is no confession of weakness so revealing as the desire to be above criticism.' But as we have seen Beveridge's recommendations were not followed, and the BBC demonstrates a continuing desire to be above criticism, employing every feint and blind to that end: appealing to its own traditions, summoning up the spectre of political control, putting on tokenism audience-reaction shows like *Talkback*, and finally attempting to head off growing political pressure for the creation of a Broadcasting Council by appointing a Complaints Commission, yet another gathering of establishment figures housed in BBC premises, at BBC expense, with narrow terms of reference defined by the BBC. The IBA has also set up a similar body for a similar purpose.

Beveridge's sensible recommendations were defeated by our national fear of change and by the massive dynamic conservatism of the BBC. But in the event the BBC received their come-uppance. Their arrogant isolation was no longer politically or socially acceptable, and so it was Selwyn Lloyd's Minority Report which was heeded. He had expressed the view that 'the only effective safeguard is competition from independent sources. Without that competition the basic evils and dangers of monopoly will remain'. ITV was created in an attempt to discipline the broadcasters by means of competition.

# Independent Television

The history of ITV demonstrates the failure of accountability through the market place. The Television Act of 1954 broke one monopoly only to create another, a monopoly of advertising revenue. If the BBC was ultimately motivated by allegiance to a political and cultural establishment, ITV's instinctive allegiance was to economic power. As Sir Hugh Greene has said, 'Commercial television is part of a country's business apparatus'.

The founding of ITV institutionalised two confusions: a confusion of the idea of competition with the idea of private enterprise finance and a confusion of advertising finance with private profit. Neither is a necessary condition of the other, but these confusions still bedevil the broadcasting debate in Britain, seriously limiting the search for alternatives, as the setting up of commercial local radio depressingly demonstrates. The confusions are at the heart of ITV's structural problems.

The ITA was established to reconcile a contradiction, a contradiction admirably defined by Pilkington: 'The Authority's task is to reconcile the two objects for which independent television is constituted and organised: two objects which do not coincide and which are, in a greater or lesser degree, opposed to one another. Because the incidental object – the sale of advertising time – is the commercial interest and duty of the companies, the natural inclination will be to pursue it as the main purpose. Their product is desirable advertising time. As commercial organisations they exist to create and sell that product; it is in their interest and duty as commercial undertakings to do so as successfully as they can . . . This private objective does not coincide with the primary and essential objective, the best possible service of broadcasting.'

According to the theory of liberal economics the commercial instinct is disciplined for the public good by competition and this aspiration was written into the Television Act. It is the IBA's duty 'to do all that they can to secure that there is adequate competition to provide programmes between a number of programme contractors independent of each other both as to finance and control'. Had the ITA been allotted two television channels at the time they would have appointed two rival companies in each area. Everyone, including the IBA in their claims for ITV2, now recognises that such direct commercial competition would produce not widened choice and higher standards but, as the experience of competition between BBC1 and ITV has shown, the scheduling of like against like in a general context of increasingly unadventurous uniformity.

In the event the Authority attempted to build competition into the system by appointing a diversity of regionally based companies rather than a few London-based giants. This regional structure remains ITV's greatest strength and the finest achievement of Sir Robert Fraser, the Director General of the ITA from 1954–1970. They also split the week between rival contractors in each area. But even this minimal amount of competition has been destroyed. The financial difficulties of the first 12 months of ITV led to the growth of networking, a procedure described by the PIB as follows: 'The planning of programmes requires co-operative arrangements between the contractors since none of the companies individually has the resources to provide all the programmes it needs and therefore a high degree of interdependence is inevitable. This work is carried out by the Network Programme Committee on which all the companies are represented, and more particularly by the Major Programme Controllers Group, consisting of programme controllers from the five network companies only (Thames, LWT, ATV, Granada and Yorkshire). Most of the detailed pre-planning, and the negotiation of programme "slots" by the network companies that often accompanies it, appear to be undertaken in this group. The significance of this procedure is that when the programmes and the producing companies are agreed by these two bodies, the companies concerned have a guarantee that the programmes will be taken by the other network companies, before production commences.' In other words ITV is run not on the basis of competition in either price or quality, but is a carve-up based on proportion of total advertising revenue. Competition in the system was further reduced in 1968 when, with the allocation of new contracts, the split week ended everywhere except in London.

Thus, without competition, it was left to the Authority to control the system in the public interest. This it has signally failed to do. The Pilkington Committee observed that 'a yet sharper criticism of the Authority implied that it had misconceived its relationship with the programme contractors; that it saw itself as advocate for them; that it excused and defended them rather than controlled them ... It is our view that while there is everything to be said for persuasion, so long as it is effective, the relationship between the Authority and the companies must be that between principals and agents. As trustees for the public interest, the Authority is answerable. It must, therefore, be master, and must be seen to be master. That the companies are widely regarded as principal and the Authority as spokesman is unsatisfactory.'

That criticism was made in 1960, but it remains true to this day, as amply demonstrated by the IBA's role in the TV4 campaign and the tone of their Annual Report which is characteristically one of justification rather than scrutiny. Thus we can see the Authority following in the footsteps of the BBC Governors and identifying inevitably with the system of which they are a part and from which they draw their identity.

But one must have some sympathy with the Authority, for, as Pilkington saw, the fault is structural. In theory they possess total power. They can refuse to transmit any item, because they control the transmitters, and they can terminate a contract at any time if in their view the Act is being infringed. The problem, as with government control, is that the stick is too big to be a realistic threat. Moreover, when it is used, as in the termination of certain contracts in 1968, it creates an instability which is against the legitimate interests of the workers in the industry, makes long-term creative planning impossible and positively encourages the companies to squeeze every last penny out of the system and diversify into safer financial areas. The government's use of the Levy as a means of controlling excessive profitability is a similarly blunt instrument. The story of LWT has shown the inadequacy of such extreme sanctions. They are ineffective because the Authority dare not use them.

In an attempt to build greater flexibility into the control of the system the Television Act was redrafted in 1964 to give the Authority greater power over scheduling. But this in no way solved the central structural problem which Pilkington correctly diagnosed as follows: 'It is not the outcome of the particular policies of those engaged in independent television; it reflects the real distribution of power in independent television behind the apparent distribution by formal constitution. The Authority's formal powers are to regulate programming in the public interest. Because the regulatory function is separated from the creative function of programme planning and production, it is negative and prohibitive. The initiative is held by the programme contractors.' This remains true. Once the Major Programme Controllers have carved up the network, it is almost impossible for the Authority to make any but minimal changes. The interlocking of programme commitments is such that, like a house of cards, pull one out and the lot come down. If the Authority asks for a programme to be removed from the schedules all it sees is a gap and a company complaining that it cannot afford to write off the investment. It has no influence over alternative programmes because it is not involved in programme choices at the ideas stage. The result is that it mandates a few prestige programmes and leaves the major part of peak-time viewing to the grossest commercial pressures. Such a system bans a programme on the politics of the Irish Republic, sight unseen, and at the same time encourages Sir Lew Grade to design series primarily for the American market, knowing that he has a guaranteed British outlet.

So if they are to have effective control the Authority is driven logically to intervene increasingly in programming. In their submission to the Minister of Posts on their plans for ITV2 the Authority admits that it 'has not attempted to control in the earliest stages the programme planning of the system' and then goes on to advocate the setting up of a Programme Planning Board which 'would provide a strong IBA presence at the centre of the system and enable the IBA to survey, at an early stage, the full range of what was available, or potentially available'. The snag is that the logic of this process does not stop there. The Authority can never stop until ITV becomes a BBC financed by advertising, totally controlled by a London-based central bureaucracy. (The present state of the BBC amply demonstrates the disadvantages of such a development. One BBC is bad enough without creating another.) Would it be better to have Brian Young making programme decisions rather than Lew Grade? One doubts it. The strength of ITV is its diversity, the very real difference in character of the companies and in some cases their strong regional identity. If that diversity is incompatible with public service so long as the companies are motivated by private profit, then it is the profit motive that must be removed. If on the other hand the country decides, through parliament, that it wants a BBC financed by advertising revenue, then they should set up such a body and stop beating the IBA for failing to reconcile the irreconcilable.

# TV Structures: Freedom or Constraint?

The debate about broadcasting in Britain has been traditionally conducted in terms of freedom. The structural problem has been seen as one of protecting broadcasting from commerce and government, the twin enemies anathematised by Huw Weldon as pap and propaganda. The desire for these twin freedoms is accurately reflected in the present structure of British Television, the BBC seen by its defenders as a bastion against commercialism, ITV seen, especially by foreigners, as freer than the BBC from government because of its 'independent' source of revenue (hence the misleading title Independent Television).

But it is more accurate to see broadcasting in terms of constraints, as a vector of conflicting pressures, as an open system that takes on its particular configuration by adapting to an environment made up externally of the public or audience, of commercial pressures and of government and internally of the broadcasters themselves. None of these pressures is of course distinct, there is a constant interaction between them. The State and the public interact through normal political channels, commerce and the public through ratings, commerce and the State via fiscal policies, the public and the broadcasters through audience research, complaints and general programme activity.

To see broadcasting in terms of constraints has certain advantages. It confronts the realities of power and control which abstract notions of freedom so easily avoid. It sees any structures as partial and temporary solutions to complex social and political problems and so is more responsive to change and less prone to pessimism than a view based on absolute notions of freedom. But above all it dethrones the broadcaster.

For the traditional debate has been conducted very much within limits set by the broadcasters. It is they who are to be freed; to do what is never very clear. Those who pursue the three great purposes of broadcasting, information, education and entertainment have assumed, as of right, the mythic mantles of their predecessors, 'freedom of the press', 'academic freedom' and 'artistic freedom'. But the stress on these freedoms has disguised the greatest constraint of all, the constraint imposed by the institutions themselves.

Pilkington illustrates well the dangers of this traditional approach: 'Though its standards exist and are recognisable, broadcasting is more nearly an art than an exact science. It deals in tastes and values, and is not precisely definable. For this reason, the formal documents could not do more than lay down general precepts and delegate to the responsible authorities the task of translating them into practices recognisable as not less than good broadcasting. It is therefore the programmes which are the test of the authorities' success . . . We had no preconceived principles by which to judge the quality of the services provided, and the constitution and organisation of the two systems. For a service of broadcasting should be judged not by the stated aims of the broadcasters but by their achievements; and it is in the light of these achievements that the structure of their organisation should be examined. We have considered first the product and then the producer, rather than the reverse. It is the listeners and viewers for whom the service is provided; and they are interested primarily in what is offered to them.'

Such an analysis sees broadcasting, not as a communication process, but as the production of packages offered to a passive audience. The value of these packages is implicitly judged by standards defined by the institutions providing them. Broadcasting becomes whatever at any time the BBC or ITV happen to be providing and 'good broadcasting' is something which, like a gentleman, can be 'recognised' by 'responsible' authorities. As the threat to healthy communication posed by those very authorities becomes every day more apparent, we begin to see the inadequacy of this analysis. Too much intellectual and moral energy, we realise, has been expended in defence of the indefensible.

It is not just in broadcasting that our inherited institutions are under attack; but what Donald Schon called in his Reith Lectures 'dynamic conservatism' ensures that in even studying our institutions, let alone criticising them and suggesting alternatives, we are faced with a huge weight of inertia, a deep-rooted fear of change. In a study of the ideological effect of school as an institution, Everett Reimer has written: 'Man has shown himself capable of creating and destroying institutions, on a planned and unplanned basis, with or without theory. At the same time he remains the prisoner of his institutions to an almost unimaginable degree. He can break his thralldom only by first understanding it thoroughly, and then by deliberately planning the renovation and replacement of his present institutional structure.

' . . . We must develop conceptual tools for the analysis of major institutions, in order to understand the historical process by which they were introduced, the sociological process by which they became acceptable, and the limitation which they now place on the search for alternatives (not only limitations of power and resources, but also limitations upon the creative imagination).'

The limitations of power and resources placed by our broadcast institutions on the search for alternatives was made very clear in the fight over the allocation of TV4 in which the IBA's most powerful and persuasive argument was always 'we are the only ones with enough studios, expertise and money to do the job'. But it is the limitations on the creative imagination which should concern us more. All over the world broadcasting is a supremely institutional process, but here in Britain our thralldom to our institutions has been particularly marked, expressed in that characteristically chauvinistic notion of British broadcasting as the 'best in the world', a notion nourished by nostalgia for the war and for the part supposedly played by the BBC in that cathartic moment of national unity and grandeur, but a notion flexible enough to clasp ITV to its ample bosom as part of the best of all possible worlds.

This hypnotic trance is probably Reith's most lasting and dangerous achievement. This submission of the process of broadcasting to the institution and to its survival and health was an achievement of which Reith was very conscious. As he wrote in *Into the Wind*, he was concerned 'less with the play and players than with setting and serving the stage'. He designed the straitjacket first and then looked around for a patient. From the start, therefore, questions of structure were of prime importance, and it is worth examining the early history of the BBC because the basic issues were the same as today's, but the reality of the institutional responses was clearer because it was as yet undisguised by myth. Moreover, by looking at a time when decisions were being made we can see that the system we have was by no means inevitable. There were then, as there remain, alternatives.

Central to Reith's notion of the BBC was the concept of authority and control. As Briggs puts it in Volume I of his *History*: 'Reith recognised the necessity of concentrating authority in a few hands. However much the constitution of the BBC changed with the years, two "cardinal principles" were maintained throughout – first that only five or six individuals were directly responsible to the Managing Directors; second, that these people, along with Reith, were in "control". A newcomer to the BBC in 1924 or 1925 could not fail to note the existence of a "core" or "stratum" of authority within the organisation . . . The BBC was not just a collection of individuals; it had a genuine corporate existence.' From the start this corporation exhibited what has remained an enduring characteristic. It was expansionist and short of money. As early as 1924 Reith wrote that, 'In some quarters it may be felt that our income is more than we require. The Board do not feel this could ever be the case. There will always be the necessity for funds for improving and extending the service.'

To what ends did Reith bend the expansionist energies of his new corporation backed by 'the brute force of monopoly'? Firstly his stress on unified central control killed the possibility of independent regional development. Technically such a regional development was inherently not only possible, but more reasonable. It was in fact difficult in the early days to maintain central control over the network of necessarily separate, relatively short-range transmitters. This anti-regional bias has remained a characteristic feature of BBC policy.

The unified central control was used for ideological purposes or, as Reith preferred to put it, the maintenance of high standards. These standards were of an essentially anti-democratic, class nature. In *Into the Wind* Reith states that had the BBC not been a monopoly it might have had to 'subordinate itself to the vote'. When the BBC talks of its independence this authoritarian tendency should be remembered. It is of a piece with Reith's successful efforts to render the Board of Governors impotent. The class nature of the BBC's standards is illuminated by a memo sent by Reith to all Station Directors in 1924: 'In some stations I see periodically men down to speak whose status, either professionally or socially, and whose qualifications to speak seem doubtful.' No nonsense about letting the lower orders speak. But not only were they not going to be given a voice, they were to hear what the controllers thought was good for them. In 1926 one of Reith's associates drafted a paper which stated that the News should be 'what those in control of the BBC think listeners should hear'. Not to put too fine a point on it, the BBC was from the start committed to censorship. This censored information was to be delivered in the bland voice of the middle class: 'We are daily establishing in the minds of the public the idea of what correct speech should be.' This policy has been described by Raymond Williams as authoritarianism with a conscience. It seems to me that the conscience was a later accretion, a mask uncomfortably worn when open authoritarianism became unacceptable.

This institution with these values had one overriding aim: its own survival. In 1932 when the BBC moved to Broadcasting House Reith told his staff that one of his main functions was 'to resist attacks on the organisation from without'. This remains the overriding motive behind the actions of senior BBC executives, the most fundamental of the system characteristics of this or any other institution. The IBA exhibits similar symptoms.

# The Institution and the Broadcaster: the system's response to its internal environment

Broadcasting is the practice of institutions and not of broadcasters, because the institution was created first and then moulded the broadcasters in its image. It is significant that a Control Board was created at the BBC before a Programme Board; broadcasters were and are, in Raymond Williams' definition, agents of the corporate image, not sources. 'A man offering an opinion, a proposal, a feeling, of course normally desires that other persons will accept this, and act or feel in the ways he defines. Yet such a man may be properly described as a source, in distinction from an agent whose characteristic is that his expression is subordinated to an undeclared intention. He is an agent, and not a source, because the intention lies elsewhere. In social terms, the agent will normally in fact be a subordinate.'

The practice of broadcasting is governed by an unwritten contract. The State says to the institution, 'You may use these frequencies to broadcast what you like, so long as you maintain standards of which we approve. These standards are to be those of the Establishment and are defined as impartiality and objectivity in factual coverage of political and social affairs and as good taste in less contentious areas.' The institution then says to its employees, 'You are responsible creative broadcasters. Feel free to broadcast as you see fit so long as you maintain the highest standards of impartiality, objectivity and good taste.' This system has, of course, become increasingly leaky as the BBC has expanded and as the creation of ITV has provided alternative sources of employment and editorial control. The Governors of the BBC and the IBA cannot personally supervise every transmission and so occasional deviations from the cultural and political consensus do get through. But such exceptional instances merely serve to highlight the reality of control, a control no less effective for being benign.

How have the institutions maintained this control? First by recruitment and promotion. The BBC in particular has recruited its producers from a narrow range of university graduates whose class background and education have already predisposed them to accept these establishment standards without question. Those who might question them can, of course, be weeded out before they can exert any dangerous influence. They are simply not promoted. The cohesion of this cultural ruling class is maintained by the creation of a gulf between producers and lesser breeds such as technicians very similar to that between officers and men in the armed services. Thus a caste is created who are convinced by the institution that they have qualities as mysterious and indefinable as the officer-like qualities so admired in the forces.

The members of this caste are then subjected to a sophisticated form of conditioning by reinforcement called 'referring-up'. This is the process by which the Director-General delegates his editorial authority to the producers working on the front-line of programme making. They are left with total freedom and are only expected to 'refer up' to their immediate superior matters upon which they are doubtful. This process gives to the producer the illusion of freedom while in fact inhibiting the exercise of that freedom. A good producer learns to avoid worrying his over-worked boss by keeping off troublesome areas. If he refers up too often he will be accused of lacking individual initiative. If on the other hand he oversteps the mark without having referred up he will be labelled as irresponsible and will rapidly, in the words of an official BBC memo on Current Affairs coverage, 'use up all his creditworthiness'.

In monopoly conditions the effectiveness of this process was reinforced by the total dependence of the broadcaster upon the institution not only for his wages but for the possibility of exercising his craft. Even since the creation of ITV there still exists a very real scarcity of outlets. Broadcasting is a small, inward-looking world in which people are well paid for doing pleasant work. Those who inhabit such a world are understandably unwilling to be expelled from it and so, while self-censorship is beginning to break down, it still remains pervasive.

Broadcasters have been induced to underwrite the legitimising myths of our broadcasting institutions because those myths have in part been designed precisely to maintain the internal cohesion of the institution and the control of those at the top by flattering the broadcaster. Isolated from his audience by the nature of his medium, the broadcaster has allowed professional standards, validated by the judgement of his peers, to become an end in themselves and a very real barrier between himself and the public. Criticism from outside the magic circle can be dismissed as ignorance. Moreover such aesthetic standards can safely be used to judge one's own and one's colleagues' work because they are apparently neutral and thus entail no wider commitment, no breach of the sacred bounds of impartiality and objectivity. Huw Wheldon, trailing behind him his reputation, born in the days of *Monitor*, as a handmaiden of the arts, has become the leading spokesman for this self-regarding definition of the broadcaster's role. 'There is no great difficulty, I believe, in actually making programmes some of which are humanist and some of which are anti-humanist, some of which are entertaining and some of which are less entertaining, some of which are more serious in this way and less serious in that. The real difficulty is how to do them well. Mediocrity is the enemy at all times . . . You've got to accept that since there are going to be difficulties of public stance it becomes more important than ever to fight against mediocrity and aim for excellence.' Thus are all the crucial issues of broadcasting policy reduced to the safely aesthetic. Moreover the aesthetic standards of judgement to be used are to be those of the very broadcasters whose practice is being judged. 'I think it awfully important to bear in mind that on the whole the good is recognisable and on the whole so is the poor. Most very good programmes have an extreme universality of acceptance. It is very rare, in my experience, for me personally to be very excited by a programme without finding that excitement shared by people whose admiration I admire next morning, and indeed by people whose admiration I do not admire. On the grounds that the good, on the whole shines and there is no mystery about it. And the deplorable on the whole shines, so that the process of doing a programme that is the best possible of its kind is not open to aesthetic convolutions.'

Any study of the history of art would show that such a statement is simply untrue. It is a perfect example of the academy attempting to impose its own standards on the whole creative world. It is not only self-regarding, but it is also defensive, implying that ignorant outsiders who do not admire the same things should go away and stop meddling in what they do not understand and what, therefore, does not concern them.

Any guilt that broadcasters might feel about the inherent élitism of this stress on 'professionalism' has been softened by the central concept of 'public service'. Raymond Williams has written illuminatingly of the essentially ideological nature of the idea of service: 'A very large part of English middle-class education is devoted to the training of servants. This is much more its characteristic than a training for leadership, as the stress on conformity and on respect for authority shows. In so far as it is, by definition, the training of upper servants, it includes, of course, the instilling of that kind of confidence which will enable the upper servants to supervise and direct the lower servants. Order must be maintained there, by good management, and in this respect the function is not service but government.' He goes on to find this ethic of service inadequate 'because in practice it serves, at every level, to maintain and confirm the *status quo*. This was wrong, for me, because the *status quo*, in practice, was a denial of equity to the men and women among whom I had grown up, the lower servants, whose lives were governed by the existing distribution of property, remuneration, education and respect. The real personal unselfishness, which ratified the description as service, seemed to me to exist within a larger selfishness, which was only not seen because it was idealized as the necessary form of a civilisation, or rationalised as a natural distribution corresponding to worth, effort and intelligence . . . The idea of service breaks down because while the upper servants have been able to identify themselves with the establishment, the lower servants have not.'

The idea of public service in broadcasting is mediated into practice through the central concepts of impartiality and objectivity. The broadcaster justifies his control over what is broadcast by claiming that he is merely the neutral holder of the ring ushering holders of all views into what is often described, by broadcasters, as 'the circle of discourse'. But he is allowed to hold this privileged position because the establishment knows that the proper exercise of impartiality and objectivity helps to maintain the *status quo*. Impartiality over Ulster, for instance, did not mean giving equal voice to the IRA and to Stormont. Objectivity, even if it could be attained, means that by holding a mirror up to nature one can only reflect what is and not what might be. Notice the way, for instance, that the arrangements for party political broadcasting reflect and therefore reinforce the political *status quo* at Westminster. Objective and impartial political coverage makes it more difficult for new voices to break into this magical circle of discourse.

There is indeed a contradiction between the two aims, a contradiction that is now rightly being exploited by the minority groups claiming access to television.

Impartiality implies a view of the world in which all views are equal and in which decisions are made after a rational consideration of all points of view. Not only does the experience of television contradict this vision, but objectivity as it is practised implies that the big battalions must be judged not on the rationality of their views but on the size and strength of their support. So we do not see Marxist and Conservative Party spokesmen pitted in equal debate, we see the consensus constantly reinforced by the careful balancing of essentially mainstream views to the exclusion of those on the fringes whose views cannot be so easily balanced. Indeed the whole notion of balance is ideological for it implies that there must always be two sides to every question. As Marx wrote of the assumed empiricism of his contemporary bourgeois economists, 'In saying that the existing relations – the relations of bourgeois production – are natural, the economists assert that these are the relations in which wealth is created and the productive forces are developed in accordance with the laws of nature. Consequently those relations themselves are natural laws, independent of the influence of time. They are eternal laws which must always govern society. Thus there has been history, but there is no longer any history.'

There are the most heartening signs in broadcasting at present that this whole system of control is beginning to break down. The outcry over 'Broadcasting in the Seventies', the blossoming of underground publications within the BBC, the protests over the censorship of news from Ulster, the call, after the media's handling of the power workers' dispute in late 1970, from members of ACTT for the setting up of a Union monitoring of TV news coverage, all these are signs that the workers in the industry are refusing to accept the legitimising myths of the institutions that employ them. This dissatisfaction has developed chiefly at the BBC, until recently the stronghold of this conditioning process. It has happened because growth and economic pressures have forced BBC management to act more like a conventional industrial concern. The cosy world of the broadcasters has been invaded by the management consultants, bringing in their train the normal conflicts of interest in industrial society between employers and employees. In particular the traditional security of employment offered by the BBC has been severely threatened, especially at the production level. Ironically the nature of central editorial control, invested in the Director-General, which is the basis for the BBC's highly hierarchical structure has made it impossible for the BBC to react to these tensions of growth as the interests of the institution might have demanded.

All organisations use an internal communication system to maintain their continued cohesion. Their need to expand places an increasing strain on these internal lines of communication and organisations solve this problem by, at certain stages of growth, splitting amoeba-like into autonomous groups. There comes a point with a 'centre-margin' structure when central control loses touch with the margins and it then has to transform itself into a network structure if it is to survive. In this regard ITV is much more flexible. The individual companies can maintain staff loyalty more easily now than the BBC. But the BBC cannot give its constituent elements sufficient independence, however many Managing-Directors it appoints, because its very existence depends upon the legitimising myth of central editorial control. For instance they were not able to make BBC 2 an independent channel, because they were driven to advocate the scheduling advantages of centralised control.

The BBC has therefore tried to solve this problem by concentrating effective editorial power in fewer and fewer hands, thus exposing the reality of central control behind the myth of producer freedom. The introduction of centralised, accurate cost control by computer, the development of scheduling techniques which stress the programme format, the series and the strand rather than the one-off programme, have made it possible to run a broadcasting service with greater effective central control. It is not often realised how few men decide what appears on BBC Television, effectively two Channel Controllers and seven Group or Departmental Heads. This process, while helping to give the BBC a unified response to external pressures, is leading within it to growing alienation, not to say anarchy. There seems now to be an irreconcilable contradiction between the BBC's size and the need for internal cohesion. To survive it must split, but it will resist this split to the last, because such a split will change its nature which rests so firmly upon the maintenance of what Reith described as 'unified standards' by means of central editorial control. Faced by this situation the broadcaster is beginning at last to question his ideological slavery.

Unfortunately the broadcasting unions have been unable fully to exploit these possibilities for change with the aim of widening editorial control by gaining for the workers in the industry a greater say in how it is run. This is in part because unions have traditionally avoided the area of programme standards and editorial control. It is also because the unions are split and in the same way as the industry. That is to say the two main unions, the ABS and ACTT, are organised largely in the BBC and ITV respectively. It is in the nature of institutions to react first to outside intervention by attempting to repulse it. This was especially true of the BBC when faced by the growth of trade-unionism. But when resistance is no longer possible, the institution moves to absorb the external aggressor into its own internal control system by a process of co-option. This has led to the ABS instinctively allying itself with the BBC and its continued existence, while ACTT, for all its battles with the employers over wages and conditions, fights for the stability and continuing existence of commercial television as, for instance, in its recent support for plans for a second ITV channel. As Donald Schon writes in *Beyond the Stable State*, 'The power of social systems over individuals becomes understandable, I think, only if we see that social systems provide for their members not only sources of livelihood, protection against outside threat and the promise of economic security, but a framework of theory, values and related technology which enables individuals to make sense of their lives. Threats to the social system threaten this framework.' Hence our thralldom to our institutions. A valuable contributory factor to breaking this thralldom in broadcasting and opening the system to change would be a unification of the existing broadcasting unions. Then the workers in the industry could fight democratically for a total transformation of the whole structure. The control of the industry by the workers on democratic lines would only be a half-way stage to full social control. It must not be allowed to halt at a slightly expanded élitism.

But it would open up the decision-making processes of the industry and begin the necessary demystification of the production process. By forcing isolated broadcasters to involve themselves fully in a political process it would help create the climate in which those broadcasters could offer their services not to the institutions and the perpetuation of their ideology, but to the public at large.

# Broadcasting and the Public

Broadcasting may indeed be a practice, not a prescription, but it is a practice carried on, as we have seen, not by individual broadcasters, but by institutions, which as open systems must adapt to their environment or die. Their relationship to the State as an external environment is in part controlled through legislation, through consciously constructed structures. Their relationship to the audience as external environment and to the broadcaster as internal environment has come under minimum structured public control. The institutions have been much freer in these areas to adapt according to their own rather than society's structural needs. Indeed it is not freedom that we want in broadcasting, but on the contrary these two areas of adaptation need to be brought under much more conscious social control. We have seen how in the absence of such control the institutions have adapted internally to the broadcasters. How have they managed their external adaptation to the audience, the public at large?

The very technical quality that makes broadcasting distinct, its ability to reach a large number of people simultaneously and instantaneously, makes for a lack of any real connection between addresser and addressee, so that the broadcaster is caught constantly between the Scylla of élitism and the Charybdis of a bogus populism, between giving the public what is good for it and giving the public what it wants. Of course the caricature view of the BBC and ITV falls into these two polarities. These two views of the broadcaster's relationship with the audience also align themselves with two contradictory views about the medium's power. The élitists legitimise their role by claiming, with Pilkington, that 'unless and until there is unmistakeable proof to the contrary, the presumption must be that television is and will be a main factor in influencing the values and moral standards of our society'. The populists defend themselves with the evidence of the social scientists that television has little measurable effect on anyone, and so, while the programmes may be trivial, it is all harmless amusement and of no great importance. Pilkington agonised over this polarity, but their alternative was merely élitism renamed 'the proper exercise of responsibility'. 'There is an area of possibility between the two; and it is within this area that the choice lies. The broadcasting authorities have certainly a duty to keep sensitively aware of the public's tastes and attitudes as they now are and in all their variety; and to care about them. But if they do more than that this is not to give the public "what someone thinks is good for it". It is to respect the public's right to choose from the widest possible range of subject matter and so to enlarge worthwhile experience. Because, in principle, the possible range of subject matter is inexhaustible, all of it can never be presented, nor can the public know what the range is.

So, the broadcaster must explore it, and choose from it first. This might be called "giving a lead"; but it is not the lead of the autocratic or arrogant. It is the proper exercise of responsibility by public authorities duly constituted as trustees for the public interest.' So long as we see broadcasting as a process of transmission by which the broadcaster delivers bits of processed experience, however 'worth while', to a passive audience, rather than as a process of involvement and inter-action to which the models inherited from traditional culture are inappropriate, we will never escape from the horns of this dilemma.

The solution found by the institutions has been to combine both approaches; to use the populist approach to legitimise and protect the irresponsible, élitist prac-tices of the institution itself. One way in which open systems adapt to external environments is by absorbing them, so as to control them. This is what the broadcasters have done to the audience. Just as the technocrats of industrial corporations have used advertising to control the consumer and so eliminate unwanted fluctuations in demand, so the broadcasters have used the statistical weapons of audience measurement and scheduling to control the audience's choices.

It seems probable that this process was an inevitable development of institu-tional broadcasting, independent of other structural considerations. That is to say, all known television networks sooner or later assume a rigid schedule pattern whether under a State, non-competitive system, under a totally commercial system, or under our mixed system. The schedule may reach its equilibrium with different assumptions about the audience built into it, but even those variations are probably contained within narrow parameters; that is to say the level of BBC2 may differ from ITV. The assumptions upon which it is planned are very similar.

A broadcasting institution is clearly forced to respond to its audience and it can only do so statistically. It is the inevitably statistical nature of the feedback in any television system that is so significant. It explains why television schedules are clear examples of Markoff chains. In the *Mathematical Theory of Communication* Warren Weaver explains the nature of a Markoff chain: 'A system which produces a sequence of symbols (which may, of course, be letters or musical notes, say, rather than words) according to certain probabilities is called a stochastic process, and the special case of a stochastic process in which probabilities depend on the previous events, is called a Markoff process or Markoff chain.' A stochastic process is created by feedback. If a system produces a random sequence of symbols, that sequence will remain random until information about the preceding sequence is fed back into the system. When this happens patterning will begin to appear in the sequence and in this case all feedback is negative, so that the pattern becomes ever more rigid until all randomness is removed. For this reason Reith was perhaps right to reject audience research; what we must search for in any broadcasting system is a way of building in randomness by means of positive feedback. Change doesn't just happen. On the contrary, because systems tend towards a steady state, change must be built in.

The broadcasting institutions were able to ignore the audience only so long as the system was expanding for other reasons. In the early days of radio and during the late 1950s in television, the explosive growth of set ownership introduced its own dynamic which dragged the institution in its wake. One suspects that the audience would have listened to and watched almost anything during those periods; that the rapid growth of TV audiences had nothing to do with the creation of ITV. What the founding of ITV did do was introduce change into the system and in such an uncertain situation extremes of programming, both high and low, were possible. The creative excitement of those years can probably be more accurately traced to the instability of the situation rather than to notions of competition, commercialism or public service.

What is undoubtedly true is that those unstable days are over. The institutions have, as far as the audience are concerned, reached a steady state in two senses. Firstly as between themselves in that the BBC and ITV split the audience more or less 50–50 and also *vis-à-vis* the viewer in that programming becomes a question of ever smaller variations on well-tried themes.

With the sophisticated scheduling techniques now available the 50–50 split is an inherent system characteristic. The ITV companies have given as one of their reasons for wanting ITV2 the fear that without it this balance will be disturbed. Such a fear stems from a fundamental misunderstanding of the system. It is not channels which compete, but institutions. BBC2 adapts to and takes audiences from BBC1. The BBC will always maintain that situation unless threatened from without, because to compete too hard with ITV would introduce instability into the system and it is not in the deepest interest of the institution to do that. Indeed to compete too hard is to invite just the response of the demand for an ITV2.

The need to control the audience rather than to serve it is a fundamental system characteristic. What competition does do is exaggerate and accelerate phenomena which are deeply engrained in a medium which can transmit messages to huge numbers of people without any possibility of having clear knowledge about who these people are and how they are reacting. However much the broadcasting institutions measure reactions, the feedback that really gets through to them is conveyed in stark and absolute terms. Either they are watching or they are not. And no communicator likes to feel that he is not being attended to.

The time characteristic reinforces the absolute nature of this choice and the institutional hysteria that thus surrounds it. Because television flows constantly the moment can never be recaptured. The TV man cannot comfort himself with thoughts of posterity or of audiences picking up or sales growing. Either they are watching tonight at 7.30 or they are not. Even a planned policy of repeats only marginally affects this truth.

Out of these pressures the characteristic method of audience control, known as scheduling, has grown. For the institution it is not the individual programme that is the message, but the whole evening's, week's, year's viewing. The schedule is the message because what scheduling has demonstrated is that size of audience delivered and the quality of the programmes are only minimally related.

What are the imperatives of this scheduling process? People tend to stay tuned to the same channel all evening. The object therefore is to make them watch yours all evening. This is known as channel loyalty and it encourages consensus television, pap, to which the minimum active response is required, because active responses are unpredictable and so may lead to audience instability, to a switch-off or to what in a competitive situation is worse, a switch-over. A schedule should flow over its audience with enough variety to satisfy the limited attention span of the human brain, but no sudden, jerky changes of gear. In this process presentation is crucial. The links between the programmes give the schedule its over-all character, hence the way in which the commercials colour the whole output of ITV, however many safeguards are built in to prevent this happening.

Given the importance of channel loyalty, the crucial moment is when people switch on for the evening. This puts steady pressure on both BBC and ITV to start their peak time pattern of viewing ever earlier. This is why protected periods for children's television, for instance, need that protection. It is significant that when the Minister of Posts finally derestricted hours in January 1972, he also ended the closed periods. It is important that in preparation for derestricted hours the companies succeeded in pressuring the IBA to move schools broadcasting out of the afternoon and into the morning. This leaves the afternoon clear for a long run up to peak time, steadily building an audience of housewives, but more importantly, making sure that the set is switched to their channel when the men come home from work. The channel that hooks them earliest lasts longest.

Having persuaded people to switch to your channel two crucial factors come into play, the inheritance factor and pre-echo. The first expresses the demonstrable truth that following a popular show a high proportion of the audience will stay to watch the next show, not out of choice but out of inertia. If the inheritance factor is based upon the habit-forming nature of all communication processes, the phenomenon of pre-echo stems from the flowing, unrepeatable nature of broadcasting. Pre-echo simply means that a significant proportion of the audience will switch to a channel in advance of a popular programme They are prepared to suffer a certain amount before it, to make sure that they don't miss the show of their choice.

# Models for a New Structure

There are many who believe that the faults of the present structure will be solved by technology. According to this view the fundamental system constraint, from which all others follow, is the scarcity of frequencies. If we had as many channels as we wanted, it is argued, there would be no need for state control and the normal action of a free society would regulate the intercourse between freely creating broadcasters and freely choosing viewers.

Such a situation does now exist in all the other fields of communication: newspapers, books, films, records, paintings, plays. These artefacts can be produced by anyone, offered to anyone, be seen by anyone. Or in theory they can. However, both the practitioners and the audience in these fields would bear witness that the practice is rather further from perfection than the advocates of multi-channel TV sometimes recognise. In all these fields the free flow of information is seriously hampered by the normal distortions of a capitalist economy at our stage of development. As Raymond Williams has put it, 'Anything can be said, provided that you can afford to say it and that you can say it profitably'.

But to recognise this is to neglect a more serious obstacle to finding a solution to our communication problems in an endless expansion, through cables, satellites and cassettes, of available channels. The obstacle is this. There appears to be in practice, as communication theory has demonstrated mathematically, an upper limit to the capacity of any communication system, and to approach even this limit requires a strict control over the flow of messages.

Broadcasting lies at the end of a long development of communication systems, a development that started with the simplest form of communication, and still the commonest, one person talking to another, and from the invention of writing onwards through printing, photography, the telegraph, film, radio and television, made it possible with each new step for one person to communicate with more and more people until with radio and television it is now in theory possible for one man to talk instantly to the whole world. Thus all communication systems beyond face to face confrontations can be seen as essentially hierarchical, means by which one can control many, and certainly these systems have enabled ever more complex, far-ranging and inclusive systems of authority to develop.

The purpose of broadcasting is to talk to large numbers of people quickly and, given the initial investment in transmitters and receivers, cheaply. The question posed by the development of cable transmission is how far can you fragment the audience before destroying the very *raison d'être* of broadcasting. Those in favour of cable TV often put forward the telephone system as an example of a democratic, free-choice communication system. But the telephone system demonstrates clearly the limits of channel capacity. The most perfect broadcast is what Norbert Wiener calls a 'to whom it may concern' message. His example is an air raid warning, and it is interesting that the telephone system is one of the ways in which we will be given the nuclear warning. At that moment the telephone system will be transformed into a broadcasting system. But 'to whom it may concern' messages are the ultimate in control. They demonstrate, indeed flaunt, a disregard of feed-back. They demand an immediate, unquestioning response. And the sending of such a message would instantly neutralise the telephone system as all numbers became simultaneously engaged. But even if telephones are left to be used by individuals, freely choosing communicators, the limitations are narrow. Only 50 per cent of subscribers can use the system to make a call at any one time, and this is the absolute ideal maximum, for it assumes that all callers will want to talk to someone different. In reality, of course, the maximum number who can freely make the call of their choice is well below this figure of 50 per cent. The possibilities of the system are not only limited by others wanting to call the same person, but by the fact that the chances of the person not being at home are also high. It should also be noted that receivers of phone calls do not exercise free choice. They merely pick up the phone when it rings. It is as though the television was locked permanently on and set to one channel.

If you start to use the phone to link one caller with many receivers the number of messages that can be passed at any one time begins to drop very fast. We can take as an example the broadcasting at present done by the Post Office over the telephone: the time, the weather, the test score, etc. These carry very small amounts of information and if the test score was expanded into a ball-by-ball commentary the phone system would soon grind to a halt, or the country would have to invest massively in a second phone in every home.

There is another limit on the capacity of a multi-channel TV system. Even with our present three-channel system we rely on old-fashioned printing and news-paper distribution to actually be able to make our choices: i.e. imagine how much real choice you could make without the *Radio Times* and *TV Times* or a newspaper. These in fact constitute a meta-language of broadcasting, and as the channels multiply the complications of choice multiply with them. Libraries present a useful comparison. They are only as useful as their catalogues, and the growth in the volume of books produced has meant that every subject now requires a bibliography so that people will know what to look for in the catalogue. Each specialised bibliography in fact narrows the span of real choice, making the widely read man into an extinct species.

We can observe the same limitations in other parallel fields of communication. The motor car offers an interesting parallel to cable TV. It too has been lauded as a bringer of choice, a provider of individual freedom. With the car one's times of arrival and departure are no longer dictated by the train or bus company. Unfortunately, as experience has shown, they are dictated much more frustratingly and unpredictably by other drivers beside whom one sits in traffic jams. Moreover the town to which you are driving becomes a wilderness of car-parks and motorway boxes. Everywhere the cry is heard: bring back public transport, for the car only brings freedom when its ownership is confined to the few. To democratise the car is to render it useless. Perhaps the same is true of broadcasting.

The same phenomenon can be observed in tourism where the tourists destroy that which they have come to see. It can be seen in the dependence of cities upon the capacity of their food distribution systems. It can be observed in politics itself, where the growing cry for a return to the grass roots is a recognition that the capacity for a national political system to handle everyone's messages without distortion is very severely limited. Indeed the two-party system exhibits many of the same characteristics as television scheduling, and for the same reasons.

It is the inherent limitation in channel capacity which leads one to regard much of the talk of freedom, when it concerns television, as romantic utopianism, and to prefer the notion of constraint. Raymond Williams writes in *Communications*: 'The democratic system, in any full sense, we can only discuss and imagine. It shares with the early commercial system a definition of communication which insists that all men have the right to offer what they choose and to receive what they choose.' Unfortunately I believe such demands are unrealistic, because if such fundamental rights, attractive as they sound, were in fact exercised, the result would be not communication but a circuit choked by 'noise'. As at a cocktail party, when everyone talks at once, you cannot even hear yourself think. I prefer therefore Enzensberger's proposition in *The Consciousness Industry*: 'Every use of the media presupposes manipulation . . . There is no such thing as unmanipulated writing, filming or broadcasting. The question is therefore not whether the media are manipulated, but who manipulates them. A revolutionary plan should not require the manipulators to disappear; on the contrary, it must make everyone a manipulator.' In other words, we must not try to isolate the media from politics, but on the contrary build political control structures more deeply into the media. In our search for such structures we have been too inhibited by equating politics, not with a process by which free men resolve their differences and work together to their mutual benefit, but with the existing structure of the State and therefore with that ruling class who control that traditional structure. That class has indeed given democracy a bad name. But even now there are other democratic structures of long standing, the Trades Union movement being the most notable example, which operate alongside and even in rivalry with that structure of representative parliamentary democracy we normally call politics.

We have seen that a television system has three distinct system parameters, its relationship with the State, its relationship to the public and its relationship to those who work within it, the broadcasters. At the moment only the first of these relationships has been politicised. The aim of this proposed model is to politicise them all, for it is just the fact that TV's relationship with the State has been structured politically that accounts for many of the imbalances in the system and for the recurrent call to keep politics out of television. What people mean when they say that is, keep the State out of television. We neither can nor should keep the State out, but we should certainly create a structure which contains countervailing political pressures.

In brief such a structure should do three things. It should open out and make explicit the State's area of control and methods of control, so that they can be scrutinised by parliament and public alike. It should allow all those who work in the industry a proper say in how it is run but finally, in order to guard against the arrogance of both State and broadcaster it must build in public representation and power at all levels, not just on top, as at present, through the parliamentary process.

As we have seen, all institutions have a tendency to resist change. How can we avoid this danger in broadcasting? How can we make the system flexible enough to respond to changing social needs rather than to the dynamic conservatism of the institution? The way is by democratising the system. Perhaps the greatest benefit of democracy is not that it allows everyone to be involved in the decisions affecting their destiny, but that it builds change into the system. It is a means, at least in theory, of managing change gently rather than violently. That is one reason why revolutionaries distrust democracy so deeply. Of course our parliamentary system doesn't allow enough change. The Chartists wanted annual elections. The Athenians allowed no one to stand for election more than once. These are both ways of building a necessary instability into the system.

All the above considerations lead one to ask for a reversal of our structural tradition. Our broadcasting institutions were imposed from the centre and have, even in ITV, which tried consciously to reverse this trend, reinforced the London-dominated tradition of British media.

I think we must build our new structures from the margins in to the centre. Central power should be minimised and peripheral power and autonomy maximised. Instead of central government appointing bodies such as the BBC Governors and the IBA, who then create a system beneath them, we should start with local broadcasting authorities, elected by and responsible to the grass-roots of broadcasting. Such a network of independent local authorities corresponds to the essentially fragmented transmission system. To cover the country with UHF television requires a grid of short-wave transmitters. It is only structural convention that assumes that these transmitters should be controlled by central authorities and in general transmit centrally originated programmes. At present the convention is for a region to opt out of this centrally provided service. This should be reversed so that the decision becomes, on the contrary, one of opting in.

How might these aspirations work out in practice? We could take as our basis the regional structure of both ITV and BBC as it now exists. This structure is at the moment undermined in ITV by networking and in the BBC has never been given a chance to develop in a system dominated by the London-based central editorial control of the Director-General. The devolution sought by Beveridge has simply never happened, and the reorganisation of 'Broadcasting in the Seventies', by creating regions with inadequate finance or facilities, increased the domination of the centre.

However, we inherit a structure of technical facilities from the present system. The BBC's English regions are based on studios in the following places: Birmingham, Bristol, Leeds, Manchester, Newcastle, Norwich, Plymouth, Southampton. In addition there are the national regions of Scotland, Wales and Northern Ireland based upon Cardiff, Glasgow and Belfast. Each of these regions is paralleled by an ITV company. Thus outside London we at present have the skeleton of a regional structure based upon eleven centres with extensive technical facilities. In each case five of these regions are major production centres.

The desire to build on this regional structure is not based upon a nostalgia for local culture, although in the so-called National regions such considerations are important. The stress on regionalism stems from a need for organisations small enough to be properly controlled by the workers within them and the society they serve. The experience of the smaller ITV regional companies shows that the public can identify with a local company in a way that is impossible with the BBC or even the major ITV companies. Moreover, if the public are to share in the democratic control of broadcasting institutions, a manageable constituency must be created. A secondary consideration is that, because objectivity is an unattainable aspiration, only a diversity of independent programme sources can hope adequately to reflect the range of views of a complex pluralist society.

In outline the structure proposed, therefore, is one of autonomous, non-profitmaking regional corporations with at least two competing in each area. These corporations would be run by a council elected 50 per cent by the workers in the corporation and 50 per cent by the local electorate. On the model of Yugoslav television this body would be responsible for the main financial and programme policy decisions. It would for instance allocate the annual budget as between programme expenditure, capital investment and wages. It would approve all schedules. It would also handle complaints, audience research and such public activities as the publication of a programme journal.

Day-to-day running of the corporation would be in the hands of a works committee elected by all the workers. This committee would take detailed decisions concerning programme planning, the buying of equipment and wage distribution. Hiring and firing would be done by a specially elected committee. The teams actually creating programmes would be as fluidly and democratically run as possible. The aim throughout should be to break down the present officers-and-men division between 'creative' producers and directors and the rest, to open up the programme-making process to public view and tear away the veil of mystification that has grown around the exercise of professional skills. All committees should meet in public and their members be subject to instant recall. All decisions should be openly fought over. Each corporation would have a Director-General elected by all the staff annually but dismissable by the public representatives on the control board.

Many broadcasters fear the close involvement of the public in the broadcasting process. They see democracy favouring timidity and even repression, with the end result rule by Mary Whitehouse. I think this is an underestimation of the public's tolerance and flexibility of mind, which we can expect when the issues have been fought out in public, the censor having to fight openly for his repression and the broadcaster openly for his freedom. It is the endemic secrecy of the present system that breeds fears both of censorship and depravity. Much of the force behind the Whitehouse movement comes not so much from disgust with programmes as from a justifiable dislike of the arrogance of broadcasters.

These regional corporations, arranged as they are in pairs in each region, would be structured into two alternative networks, each of approximately seven corporations. The corporations in each network would elect a national network committee to regulate programme exchanges between members and to run a London-based News and Current Affairs service. They would also act as a final court of appeal for public and staff complaints, having the right when necessary to demand airtime to rectify a complaint of suppression by a programme maker or misrepresentation by a member of the public. Bodies who felt that their views were not being heard on the air could also process their complaints up to National level, where they could be granted airtime.

The third available network would be run by a separate body as a national channel based on London and using some of the excess capacity there. This body, perhaps called TV3, would consist of appointed government representatives, elected representatives of the Unions at present in the Federation of Broadcasting Unions, and representatives of the public probably elected via the boards of the regional corporations. It would be a condition of membership of all control bodies throughout the system that the duration of office should be three years and no one should be eligible for reelection. Every effort should be made to stop the perpetuation of élites even at some cost in efficiency. The body running this national channel should first be responsible for scheduling this channel and running a news service. It would also co-ordinate all transmission facilities in the country. It would take over the functions of the Television Advisory Committee and as well as being responsible for looking into the technical future would also sponsor general television research. It would act as a permanent Committee and as well as being responsible for looking into the technical future would also sponsor general television research. It would act as a permanent Comworks. It would do this by originating no programmes of its own except the news service, but by putting its facilities at the disposal of creative groups who were outside the regional structure. Its meetings would of course be public, its decisions openly arrived at and available for public scrutiny.

# Post-Annan Postscript

The original version of this monograph was written, as the Introduction makes clear, in an atmosphere of potential, and indeed over-delayed, change in our inherited broadcasting structures. At that time many, both inside and outside broadcasting, put much faith in the radical possibilities of a Committee of Inquiry and actively campaigned, against Government opposition and inertia, for such a committee to be set up.

Such campaigning was always in part tactical, namely an attempt to get the Government of the day either to act more forcefully, for instance upon the recommendations of the Select Committee on Nationalised Industries report on the IBA, or to stop the Government acting, for instance over ITV2 or commercial radio. Nonetheless, mixed with such tactical manoeuvering of mixed political motives and perspectives was a strand of liberal belief in an inquiry for its own sake as a way of letting the people into the debate on the future of British broadcasting. Such faith was always naive and now that such a Committee has deliberated and reported can be seen to have been misplaced. As the post-Annan debate, such as it has been, has shown more clearly than the report itself, the mood has decisively changed to one of a weary and fatalistic acceptance of the *status quo*.

In part this is because of a general shift in economic climate which makes an expansion of broadcasting, as a catalyst of structural change, even more obviously unrealistic than it always was. But the work of the Annan Committee itself has also contributed in a major way to the changed mood. Indeed it is possible to sustain the cynical argument that Annan, like all such Committees of Inquiry, was expressly designed to lance the boil of radical discontent (and in particular to head off proposals for radical reform from within the Labour Party itself) by allowing all voices to express themselves in evidence to the Committee, there to be nullified, because by their nature unstructured and unfocussed, by the 'on the one hand and on the other' of committee compromise. Certainly what the Annan Committee has done is, paradoxically, to discredit structural change by partially endorsing it. That is to say, in the Report one can find support for a range of structural changes ranging through varying degrees of radicalness: the splitting up of the BBC, a new authority to run local radio, the kernel, at least, of a permanent Broadcasting Commission in the proposal for a Telecommunication Advisory Committee and a Public Enquiry Board for Broadcasting, and a general support for more public involvement in the running of our broadcasting services.

But these proposals for change are presented piece-meal, not as part of a coherent strategy for a coherent system. This lack of a coherent strategy is closely linked to the Annan Committee's clear decision in favour of compromise, whereby in order to avoid facing their disagreements to the point of an open political split expressed in majority and minority reports, they chose to let a thousand individual reservations bloom. Whether this compromise led to the glaring absence of a coherent strategy (an absence justified as 'pluralism') or vice-versa is immaterial. The result has been the studied avoidance of the hard choices which must lie behind any proposals for structural change, so that when others have begun to examine Annan's proposals for an Open Broadcasting Authority or a Local Broadcasting Authority, the proposals have dissolved under the pressure of the real contradictions which the Annan presentation was designed to avoid, but which in the real world will not go away. To give just one example; one Annan recommendation is that 'So far as possible, each Broadcasting Authority should have its own source or sources of revenue and should not compete with other Broadcasting Authorities for exactly the same source of revenue'. This recommendation is in line with the general desire to avoid political control of broadcasting via control over financial allocation. However, the Report then proposes a Local Broadcasting Authority which, since it is to combine commercial and BBC local radio, will either be competing with ITV and the Report's proposed OBA for advertising revenue as well as needing a proportion of the licence revenue (and in that case who is to decide what proportion?) or will need direct subvention out of public funds, thus not only raising the spectre of direct political control (elsewhere judged intolerable for the financing of the BBC) but also competing once again with the OBA, which is also to receive public funding to supplement its advertising revenue. Thus in its LBA and OBA proposals Annan simply avoids articulating the real and linked financial and institutional choices and by so doing has contributed to a general feeling that all proposals for structural change are naive and unrealistic, a feeling powerfully reinforced, of course, by the publicity machines and political lobbyists of the existing power holders in broadcasting.

Thus an opportunity for change has been lost. It can of course be argued that such a possibility never existed; that the considerable body of evidence put to Annan in favour of change was mere spitting in the wind; that Annan, given the present balance of political forces in Britain, could only fulfil the role which with hindsight it can be seen to have actually performed, namely to further legitimise the *status quo*.

Clearly at one level this was not the Annan Committee's intention. The members explicitly state that they 'do not believe that the present structure of broadcasting, which was devised to meet the needs of the 1960s, will be adequate to meet the demands of the 1980s' and, as I have pointed out, they make a number of proposals for structural change, including a minority report advocating something as radical in British terms as the institutional separation of BBC TV and BBC Radio. And as the existence of ITV should constantly remind us, minority reports are sometimes acted upon.

It is proper also to recognise a shift in emphasis in Annan as compared with Pilkington towards structural concerns. 'Those who point out', they say, 'that the output of individuals is to some extent conditioned by the structure of the industry in which they work, are not wrong'. But as the half-hearted terms of that recognition demonstrates, the approach of the Annan Committee to structural reform was bound to be abortive because they remain trapped within the traditional perspective of romantic individualism and of freedom for the broadcaster. In the end once again they have allowed the broadcaster to define the terms of the debate.

'We do not agree', they state, 'with those who have suggested that the concern of the Pilkington Committee for good programmes was somehow misconceived and that the real issue is the control of broadcasting. . . . On the contrary we regard the programmes as unquestionably the most important – and arguably the only – test of any broadcasting system.' (Section 3.23.) And they go on to say in a later section of the Report: 'Programmes are made by the people who create them, and creation does not express itself through the rational application of rules, guide-lines or regulations. Necessary as they may be, these safeguards are merely filters in the imaginative process and brakes on the creative impetus.' (Section 4.23.)

Such an endorsement of producer ideology leads directly to an almost anarchist view of structure as inherently evil. Such a view stems directly, of course, from classical liberal ideology, but the recognition of its centrality in the Annan Report does lead us to an over-arching structural question within which the debate concerning broadcasting structures should be seen and which was neglected in the first edition of this monograph. This is the question of the relation between civil society and the State. Liberal ideology sees civil society as the weakly structured source of human happiness and human good to be defended against any encroachment by the State, the role of which is seen minimally as holding the ring. From within such a position no realistic theory of the State is possible, for it is seen as undifferentiated evil. Ironically the Marxist position, marked by the same Rousseauesque inheritance, shares the same weakness, namely an unwillingness or an inability to face the problems of the State, not only in bourgeois democracies but in any complex, structured social totality. Thus Annan misrepresents politics and bureaucracy, making no distinction between the different actual or potential roles of Executive, Legislature or Civil Service and implicitly regarding broadcasting institutions as organisations without bureaucracies. Thus while, in attacking proposals for independent research, it observes that 'so many of the fundamental decisions which have to be taken are political', it at the same time wishes to keep politics out of broadcasting. While arguing against a Broadcasting Council on the grounds that it will duplicate 'the work of those in his Department [The Home Secretary's] whose duty it is to advise him', it at the same time constantly expresses a generalised fear of bureaucracy. This use of complex terms as simple swear words is perfectly exemplified when Annan warns that 'the price to pay for a Broadcasting Commission would be rigidity, limitation of choice, a threat to freedom of expression and of political interference and spreading bureaucratisation'.

But ironically Annan's endorsement of producer ideology also leads to misrepresentation of the role of broadcasters as well. This is well illustrated when the Report writes, 'the contention that the over-weaning power of the broadcasters who "set the agenda" and "define reality" for the public and "structure the view between governors and governed" must be curbed, while at the same time the individual producer is to be granted far greater freedom, seems to us a mysterious paradox'. (Section 3.23.) This only seems a paradox if one fails to differentiate within the category 'broadcaster' between broadcasting management and the interests and function of the broadcasting institution on the one hand, and the individual broadcaster on the other, with the two in a complex dialectical, structured relationship. But such a recognition would force Annan to recognise, as it fleetingly does in its consideration of the BBC, that bureaucracy necessarily exists within broadcasting as well as outside and that to endorse the existing Authorities and structure of Ministerial authority is merely to endorse an existing bureaucracy against a possible alternative. It is not to endorse creative freedom against bureaucracy.

But to be against bureaucracy is merely silly. Bureaucracy is a necessary and creative part of our social process. TV broadcasting is carried out by organisations of a necessary minimum financial, administrative and technical complexity. These institutions employ individual broadcasters to make individual programmes. But these programmes are part of series and schedules, which are in turn part of budgeted financial plans. Far from being a brake on the creative process, the bureaucracy which organises and controls the cash flow, the capital investment, the technical development and purchasing, the staff hiring and training, not to mention the long term programming policies, is the indispensable foundation for any creative practice within television. And it is to these over-all policy areas, controlled as they must be by bureaucracies, that public decision making needs to be directed.

This failure to distinguish between the area of creative individual or small-team decision making and the area of over-all structural control within a broadcasting organisation leads to the reiterated fear, expressed by Annan every time it examines proposals for the setting up of bodies designed to take policy-making outside the closed arena of the broadcasting institution and place it within a more overtly politicised public domain, that it will lead to day-to-day political interference. Whereas the opposite is more likely to be the case. Since day-to-day interference by politicians is inherently difficult the price of political embarrassment in an open system is always likely to be higher than the results conceivably achievable. While anyway we know that the real political control of information by politicians and civil servants is exercised not by interfering in the sphere defined as the media's own and thus vigorously defended beneath the banner of freedom of the press, but on the contrary by rigid control at the source of information, namely within government itself.

But perhaps the greatest weakness of the Annan Report is one shared by my original monograph, namely a neglect of economic structures. In the case of Annan such neglect is part, of course, of their liberal ideology and their accompanying belief in the largely unproblematic nature of civil society. This neglect of economic structures is, once again, ironically shared by many currently fashionable variants of a Marxist critique of the media, which effectively nullify the materialist determinants of economic structure beneath an over-arching idealist notion of discourse or ideology. In Annan's case this neglect of economics leads them into simply assuming that sufficient funds will be forthcoming to sustain the level of programme quality they desire, to neglecting both the structural dynamics of a system based upon a clear split between advertising and public finance at a time when public expenditure is being rigorously held down, and also the effects of television being very much part of a world economy. For instance, much of the quality of British TV, not to mention levels of employment, etc., can be directly related to the high proportion of home produced material. Both the BBC and ITV undertake to keep foreign material below 12 per cent of total output. At a time when TV, for general economic reasons related to its high proportion of labour costs, is becoming relatively more expensive, TV networks throughout Europe are under growing financial pressure, which can be met either by cutting programme budgets or by both exporting and importing programmes. In both cases costs are kept down by being spread over a larger market. The effect of both processes is to significantly alter the TV service received by the viewer.

Another response to this problem is to reduce the amount of TV, thus concentrating a given national expenditure on fewer programme hours. Given that Britain already has more TV than its comparable European neighbours, most of whom are now also richer, a cut back in the service would seem to be an eminently rational proposal. It is nowhere even discussed by the Annan Committee, for to do so would be both to question the delicately balanced competitive *status quo* and also to destroy the one chance of being able both to pander to the broadcasters and make apparently radical proposals for structural change. For this chance depends upon expansion, since Annan was unwilling to mount a structural assault on the heartland of British broadcasting. The broadcasters favour a Fourth TV Channel because to rank and file producers it appears to offer more work and to broadcasting managers it offers a solution to the problem of a system with a static or declining work force and thus limited possibilities of promotion or of recruiting new talent. To the financial interests behind ITV it offers further opportunities for profitable investment in an expanding private sector of broadcasting. Disagreement among broadcasters starts over what exactly is to be done with the Fourth Channel. Annan favours a Fourth Channel because it can notionally be asked to do all the desirable things not at present done by the other channels, without looking too closely at why existing channels cannot or will not do these things. In particular, in line with Annan's general thinking the OBA is going to encourage diversity, pluralism and creative freedom by being structure-less. This improbable feat is achieved precisely, as its critics have rightly and with some well-directed ribaldry pointed out, by giving the new Authority no conceivably realistic source of funds. For of course had Annan clearly designated the purse-strings, they would also have delineated the sources of structural power. While such sources of power may not act directly upon an independent broadcasting authority, they will broadly constrain the actions of that authority. It will be more directly in the interests of the controlling bureaucracy to satisfy those sources of power than others. Annan's case for expansion is based upon an unexamined notion of 'demand for new services', when so far as we know at all, from surveys conducted by the Centre for Mass Communication Research at Leicester University, there is no public demand whatsoever for a Fourth Channel. But if, in spite of this, one accepts, as I do not, the case for expansion, then it can only be funded either out of advertising revenue or out of public funds. If Annan had accepted the case for public funding, its members would have been forced to re-examine their whole attitude to the question of the relation of such funding to political control and would then have been forced to re-examine their support for the Licence fee as the proper method of funding public broadcasting; for whatever the mechanism used for raising public funds for broadcasting, decisions would have to be taken on some comparative basis as to the relative amounts within the proportion of public expenditure going to broadcasting, going to the BBC and the OBA, and in the area of radio to the LBA. If on the other hand Annan had fully examined the implications of funding the Fourth Channel from advertising revenue, they would have been forced to question not only the way in which ITV is at present financed, which in notable and regrettable contrast with Pilkington they fail to do, but also how competition for advertising would be regulated between ITV and the OBA. This would in its turn have led them to a recognition that a series of notionally independent Authorities with notionally independent sources of revenue is a comforting myth, that existing and any future additional services compete for a limited proportion of GNP within an increasingly competitive international environment, that provision of a diverse service of high quality requires central regulation by a policy-making body of just that sort against which they have resolutely closed their minds. The end result of Annan's OBA proposal has been to make it more likely that ITV2, which they specifically and rightly did not want, will come to pass.

Following Annan's failure the case for structural change still has to be made. Such a case needs to explicitly recognise the severe economic constraints upon the size of a TV system and reject expansion as a solution to TV's structural dilemmas. It needs to explicitly reject the 'civil society versus State' dichotomy which, unacknowledged, still governs consideration of the relationship between broadcasting and the State. It needs to recognise the distinction between the broadcaster as individual creator and the broadcaster as a functional part of an institutional system for providing a continuous broadcasting service, a system within which the creative act is necessarily embedded and by which it is continuously and massively conditioned and it needs to do this without collapsing into a denial of all individual human agency. While recognising that the relationship between the individual viewer and the individual programme is an important and irremovable moment in the cultural process of television, it needs also to recognise that it is not and cannot be individual consumer choice that governs the provision of a programme service nor can the audience usefully be conceived as a plurality of atomised individuals who, in the words of Annan, 'expect their own view to be expressed in one form or another'.

It follows from this, in my view, that scarce broadcasting funds require centralised allocation. It is the quantity of the funding and the nature of the funding source that is the most fundamental determining constraint on a broadcasting structure. If through fear of political control you reject, as Annan does, increased public funding for broadcasting, you immediately, as Annan effectively does, hand broadcasting over to increased control by private capital. It is this most fundamental structural choice that Annan never articulates.

The economics of broadcasting exhibit one key characteristic. The consumers only pay directly for reception. But since this represents approximately 70 per cent of total spending on broadcasting, there is one crucial consequence. The public, having invested in reception, has contracted not for individual programmes, its preference for which it cannot record directly through the market, but for a service. This concept of a service in its turn implies a continuous and considerable financial commitment.

Because the State controls, as a scarce public resource, access to the means of broadcasting, and thus controls the over-all structure of the broadcasting economy, it implicitly assumes and in all countries has assumed, however indirectly, responsibility for the funding of the services whose existence it has willed.

The means by which and the extent to which this responsibility has in fact been fulfilled in Britain is precisely the problem. Many of the BBC's financial problems can be traced back to the State's willing of BBC2 and of colour without providing adequate funding. The history of ITV and of ILR shows that where there is a conflict between the requirements of the relevant Act and solvency, solvency triumphs.

Any financial structure for broadcasting needs to take into account the following factors:

(a) Broadcasting is a unified economy, because even with differing sources of revenue, broadcasting networks compete for audiences, for broadcasting talent, for purchased programmes and for programme sales.

(b) That broadcasting is also intimately linked to other areas of the media industry. This tendency for all media industries to become a closely interlinked economic system will affect the broadcasting economy whether you have a private sector within it or not, but the effects will clearly be greater so long as there is a private sector within broadcasting.

(c) That a distinction needs to be made between investment in a broadcasting infra-structure, such as transmitters, studios, etc., and investment in programme production, for two reasons. They require a different planning time-scale and they need to be considered differently from the point of view of political control. It has been made clear, for instance by Roy Jenkins when he was Home Secretary, that the Government quite properly intervenes in the BBC's capital planning programme when renegotiating the licence. No doubt similar considerations are borne in mind more indirectly when the level of the Levy is being negotiated.

(d) That the over-all quality of a nation's broadcasting service is closely related to the money invested in it and that this closely relates in its turn to the level of GNP.

(e) That the over-all cost of a broadcasting service of a given quality is not an arcane mystery locked within the soul of the creative broadcaster, but can be calculated with relative ease at any given time and is so calculated by the planners within broadcasting institutions or programme companies. Annan's failure to do this in relation to their proposed OBA is a significant weakness.

(f) That the State already intervenes in the economy of broadcasting in the following ways:—

Via the BBC by deciding, at present on an annual basis, the level of the Licence fee and by associated confidential agreements on capital expenditure and, for instance, through pay policy.

Via the IBA by (1) creating a monopoly of TV advertising, (2) by controlling the amount of advertising that can be carried, (3) by controlling or removing control from broadcasting hours, (4) by controlling advertising rates through the Price Commission, (5) most directly by means of the Levy.

I would argue that all the above factors point to the need for a central Executive Broadcasting Commission to collect and allocate funds for British Broadcasting from whatever source they may be drawn.

I myself continue to favour the complete abolition of advertising finance within broadcasting, but I recognise that such a proposal is simply utopian at present. But if one accepts advertising as a source of revenue, one certainly should not be led, as Annan has been, into accepting the existing structural split between a private enterprise network financed by advertising and a public network financed out of public funds. By accepting such a structural split Annan was nowhere able to look at the over-all problem of the financing of broadcasting and its members were so blinded by the *status quo* that they were able to claim that they had 'not uncovered any evidence of concentrations of power which are deliberately perverting the use of frequencies to their own ends', when not only is one TV network specifically devoted to private profit maximisation, but on that network specific amounts of airtime are set aside for advertisers to use for their own purposes, the only social group so privileged. This privilege is particularly marked when compared to the scanty amount of time allowed to established political parties. Thus while I unwillingly accept advertising, I do not accept the need for a private enterprise element in broadcasting. While it could be argued that such a structure was necessary in order to facilitate the generation of private capital investment to start the ITV system, it is now a solid and immovable part of our broadcasting structure to which the present private enterprise structure with its farago of contracts is entirely inappropriate.

But one of the reasons that Annan's presentation of the OBA is so inadequate is that it proposes a mix of advertising and public funds and then fails to consider the mechanisms for arriving at the over-all level or appropriate mix of these two funding sources. However, this they could not do for had they done so they would have been forced to admit that it was possible to have as part of our broadcasting structure a body capable of:—

(a) negotiating directly with the Government for public funds

(b) relating public funding explicitly to levels of advertising funding and to mechanisms for controlling that level.

This would in its turn have inevitably brought into question the level both of the BBC's and of ITV's existing level of funding and the mechanisms for their collection and distribution.

It should be noted that if the BBC were to be split up, as a minority of the Annan Committee recommends, and were an LBA to be set up, someone would have to decide how existing public funding, i.e., the Licence revenue, was to be distributed between these various bodies. Once again this is a problem Annan simply avoids, since to face it would throw into question its whole anti-structural, anti-State planning philosophy.

So in brief I believe that, largely for financial reasons, Britain requires a central Executive Broadcasting Commission, playing a similar role in relation to broadcasting as that played by the Universities Grants Commission in relation to Universities. It would agree with Government both long-term capital plans and the public input into production, probably on some rolling budget basis, although I cannot see myself why broadcasting should be made any less susceptible to the general political pressures on public expenditure than the Health or Education services. It is certainly strange that we accept with barely a murmur the excessive fluctuations of advertising revenue while wishing at the same time to protect broadcasting from similar, and indeed related, fluctuations in the flow of public funds.

Such a Commission should be composed of representatives of the constituent broadcasting organisations, of public representatives and of appointees of the responsible Minister in equal proportions. The public representatives could be arrived at by a variety of means. They could come up through local and regional broadcasting councils, they could be nominated by interest groups such as the CBI, TUC, etc., by political parties, by associations of viewers and listeners as proposed by Marghanita Laski and Philip Whitehead in the Annan Report. It has to be admitted that this whole area of democratic representation on public bodies is fraught with difficulty. What is noticeable is that such institutional research and experiment is scandalously neglected in comparison with, for instance, technical or economic research, while it may in fact be more vital. This whole problem is dealt with in much more detail in the companion volume in this series, *Broadcasting and Accountability*, by Caroline Heller.

Such an Executive Commission should have powers similar to those now exercised by the IBA to co-ordinate scheduling, to control the amount of advertising and the rates. It should not, however, hold the IBA's present powers over programme content, which should be exercised at the level of the broadcasting organisation. Each broadcasting network or individual regional or local broadcasting organisation, as the case may be, should be run by a board of Governors jointly representative of public and broadcasters and fully responsible within the budgets and scheduling framework laid down by the Broadcasting Commission for their output within whatever broad constraints, such as those of existing Acts or Charters, Parliament may choose to impose. Such constraints need not be uniform. For instance, the French model might be followed, as indeed Annan hints it should be; in this each broadcasting organisation is given specific and different goals and obligations. But, and this is the crucial point, financial strategy and allocation would be clearly separated from detailed programme policy.

As I said earlier Annan, in its general dislike of bureaucracy and so-called political interference, fails to distinguish between the structural problems of executive co-ordination focussed crucially around finance and the wider problems of policy debate and advice. As I outlined in my original monograph, there is a tendency for broadcasting institutions to be, like all institutions, self-defensive. The Executive Commission would be no exception. Thus there is a need for a parallel body, explicitly without executive authority, to act as the system's watch dog: a National Broadcasting Policy Council.

Such a Council would need to combine the function of Annan's proposed Telecommunications Advisory Committee and the proposed Public Enquiry Board. Annan's notion that you can separate technical and social policy implications is unrealistic. It is precisely their interaction that is increasingly crucial. Nor would it be necessary, as Annan assumes, for the telecommunications manufacturing industry and the major users such as broadcasters and the Post Office to be represented on such a body as has indeed been past practice. Such a Policy Council would be able to gather the best informed evidence and advice from these sources without their actual representation on the Council. It is indeed the need for a strict separation of policy advice from executive authority and interest that needs stressing. It is significant that Annan's consideration of the role of research completely misses this central structural point. The Report states in Section 6.25:

'Some of us are sceptical whether research which is not commissioned by those responsible for decision taking is likely to be of direct use in making policy decisions. The model, which envisages a research team asking the broadcasters for the relevant information and then informing them by an analysis of that information what policy decisions should be taken, seems misconceived.'

This appears to disregard the lessons both of management consultancy and of that separation of powers whereby a Legislature supervises an Executive; namely that it often is those responsible for executive decisions who are most blinded by the narrow parameters and precedents of their institutional fields of action, so that it is, precisely, only outsiders who can ask the relevant questions and make sure they get the relevant information.

Such a Policy Council would advise the responsible Minister but would itself have no executive powers. Its influence would rest on the thoroughness with which it conducted investigations and encouraged public debate and upon the ability to publicise what it saw as abuse. It would indeed take over many of the powers at present exercised by civil servants inside the Home Office. Annan seems to fear such a possibility (a sign of its conservatism) but it is only by prizing areas of policy formulation out of the existing confines of Whitehall that more open and efficient government will result, as is now being realised painfully in many areas.

To sum up briefly, the problem of the optimal social use of scarce broadcasting resources can only be solved by the creation of a central executive authority with over-all responsibility for financial allocation. The problems of a system in which policy formulation takes place behind the closed doors of institutions with deeply vested interests in the *status quo* can only be solved by a permanent and independent, non-executive Policy Council. Such a structure will make broadcasting more responsive to the will of the people as expressed through Parliament and through the Policy Council enable public representatives to play a fuller and more regular part in the discussion of broadcasting policy. Within such a structure programme policy could be made more responsive both to the individual broadcasters and to public groups, by restructuring subsidiary broadcasting authorities to give both broadcasters and public a greater say in their management.

Such a structure would allow for the more open expression and interplay of those conflicting interests and structural constraints that must exist within any broadcasting system. Broadcasting can never be free. The choice lies between constraints openly planned and consciously accepted and constraints imposed and unconsciously accepted.

# Bibliography

Bakewell, Joan and Garnham, Nicholas, *Television: The New Priesthood*, Allen Lane, 1970.

Briggs, Asa, *The History of Broadcasting in the United Kingdom*, Oxford University Press, 4 vols., 1961, 1965, 1970, 1978.

Briggs, Asa, *Governing the BBC*, BBC Publications, 1979.

Burns, Tom, *The BBC: Public Institution and Private World*, Macmillan, 1977.

Curran, Gurevitch and Woollacott (eds.), *Mass Communication and Society*, Edward Arnold for the Open University, 1977.

Timothy Green, *The Universal Eye — World Television in the Seventies*, The Bodley Head, 1972.

Greene, Sir Hugh, *Third Floor Front*, The Bodley Head, 1970.

Groombridge, Brian, *Television and the People*, Penguin, 1972.

Hood, Stuart, *A Survey of Television*, Heinemann, 1967.

*Intermedia*, journal of the International Institute of Communications.

Open University Course Units 10 & 11, on Media Organisations.

*Report of the Broadcasting Committee* 1949 (Beveridge Committee), HMSO Cmnd. 8116, 1951.

*Report of the Broadcasting Committee* 1960 (Pilkington Committee), HMSO Cmnd. 1753, 1962.

*Report of the Committee on the Future of Broadcasting* (Annan Committee), HMSO Cmnd. 6753, 1977.

*Second Report from the Select Committee on Nationalised Industries*, Session 1971-72, sub-committee B, HMSO House of Commons paper 465.

Simon of Wythenshawe, *The BBC From Within*, Gollancz, 1953.

Smith, Anthony, *The Shadow in the Cave*, Allen & Unwin 1973; Quartet, 1976.

E. G. Wedell, *Broadcasting and Public Policy*, Michael Joseph, 1968.

E. G. Wedell (ed.), *Structures of Broadcasting; A Symposium*, Manchester University Press, 1970.

Williams, Raymond, *Communications*, Penguin, 1970.

Williams, Raymond, *The Long Revolution*, Penguin, 1965.

Williams, Raymond, *Television: Technology and Cultural Form*, Fontana, 1974.

Wyndham Goldie, Grace, *Facing the Nation: Television and Politics 1936-76*, Bodley Head, 1977.